OPENING *the* SCRIPTURES

A Guide *to the*

Catechism

for use with the

Sunday Readings

OPENING the SCRIPTURES

A Guide to the
Catechism
for use with the
Sunday Readings

Reverend Kris D. Stubna, S.T.D.
Secretary for Education, Diocese of Pittsburgh

OUR SUNDAY VISITOR PUBLISHING DIVISION
OUR SUNDAY VISITOR, INC.
HUNTINGTON, INDIANA 46750

+ Contents

+ Preface

At every Sunday liturgy, we have an opportunity to hear the Word of God and to respond to the challenges of the Gospel reflected in the living teaching tradition of the Church. We come together to experience the saving message of Jesus Christ.

Yet there are many faithful Catholics, especially some young adults who can be described as "undercatechized," who come to Mass and receive their only instruction and teaching about the Faith in the liturgy through its pedagogical aspect, and particularly in the homily.

The Lectionary readings at Mass present us with an enormous opportunity. The early Church, in its desire to capture in written form the story of Jesus and the impact of his death and Resurrection in our lives, wrote and compiled what we now know as the New Testament. The Church also recognized those writings that we refer to as the Old Testament. The challenge to us in the twenty-first century is to understand those readings as they reflect two millennia of the Spirit-filled teaching of the Church. The Body of Christ is a living reality, and the teaching of the Church reflects a living, deepening understanding of the Word of God and its application to our lives.

In addition to the Lectionary and its three-year Sunday cycle of readings covering most of the Bible, we also have as a resource the *Catechism of the Catholic Church*, an authoritative and complete compendium of our Catholic faith.

Opening the Scriptures is intended to assist us as we attempt to unfold the richness of God's Word in the context of Sunday liturgy using both the readings and the *Catechism of the Catholic Church*. This is a particularly helpful tool for all priests and deacons in homily preparation, but valuable to every Catholic. In the readings at Mass we have the inspired Word of God taken from the books of the Old Testament, the writings of the New Testament, and particularly the four Gospels. In the *Catechism of the Catholic Church* we have, in the words of Pope John Paul II, a "new, authoritative exposition of the one and perennial apostolic faith" that "will serve as a 'valid and legitimate instrument for ecclesial communion' and as a 'sure norm for teaching the faith' " (apostolic letter *Laetamur Magnopere*, approving and promulgating the *Catechism of the Catholic Church*).

All of us have been called in some way to be teachers of the Word; nothing should distract us from this significant ministry. From the beginning of the Church's life, preaching the Word of God has enjoyed an urgency and centrality of importance. "It is not right that we should give up preaching the word of God to serve tables" (Acts 6:2).

We are aware that when we give a homily, or when we share the light of faith with another, it is not our wisdom, our words, or our understanding that we communicate to God's people. Rather, we are witnesses to the message of the Church, proclaiming the Word of God as it is held in continuity with the apostles. We speak nothing other than the revelation of Christ and the teaching of his Church.

To help all of us more readily access the wealth of the Church's teaching as it is rooted in the words of Sacred Scripture, *Opening the Scriptures* takes the major themes of the *Catechism of the Catholic Church* and identifies where in the three-year Lectionary cycle these principal teachings can be found. It then brings the two together in a way that allows us

PREFACE

faithfully, authentically, and fruitfully to develop the seeds so richly found in the Scriptures, in a way that applies the lived teaching experience of two millennia.

My hope is that this book will help enrich our faith and understanding in the breadth and width, the depth, beauty, and astounding coherence of the teaching of Christ and his Church. *Opening the Scriptures* is meant to help us to a richer understanding of all that God has revealed, that Christ has so fully explained, and that his Church continues to teach and to apply in a living, life-giving tradition today.

MOST REVEREND DONALD W. WUERL, S.T.D.
Bishop of Pittsburgh

+ *Introduction*

This project, *Opening the Scriptures*, seeks to serve several purposes.

First, it can help the homilist in his preparation for the task of preaching. The Instruction on the Proper Implementation on the Sacred Liturgy, *Inter Oecumenici* (September 26, 1964), allows for the development of a plan for preaching (a syllabus) to assist in the systematic presentation of the Church's teachings throughout the liturgical year. By using the *Catechism of the Catholic Church* as the compendium of the Church's teaching, this project has identified all the major catechetical themes of the Church necessary for the life of faith. At the same time, over the course of the three-year cycle of the Lectionary, this project shows it is possible to connect these catechetical teachings with the liturgical and biblical themes of the readings.

The word "homily" is given a wide range of definitions both by popular dictionaries as well as the Church's teachings and her practice. For some, the homily is a biblical sermon; for others, a doctrinal talk. Some claim its purpose is to edify its learner, while others say it should instruct people in faith and morals.

The Second Vatican Council restored the biblical form of preaching and gave to the liturgical homily "the foremost place" (*Dei Verbum* 24). Conciliar and post-conciliar teaching emphasized the importance of the homily in the liturgy as well as the diversity of understanding concerning its purposes. In *The New*

Dictionary of Sacramental Worship, edited by Peter E. Fink, S.J. (Liturgical Press, pp. 553-558), homiletic preaching in the section "Homily" is defined in its fullest sense in four ways:

It must be biblical. As *Dei Verbum* 21 asserts, "all the preaching of the Church must be nourished and ruled by Sacred Scripture." Preaching is to draw its content from the Sacred Scripture and liturgical sources. The preacher must, in every way possible, "break open" the Word for the congregation.

It is profoundly liturgical. Acting as the unifying force connecting the Liturgy of the Word and the Liturgy of the Eucharist, a homily should expound the meaning of the liturgical readings in a way that leads to an active participation in the Eucharist. How often the great homilies of the Church Fathers were mystagogical — inviting the congregation to the mysteries of Christ celebrated in the Eucharist. As *Sacrosanctum Concilium* 33 said, "Although the sacred liturgy is above all things the worship of the divine majesty, it likewise contains much instruction for the faithful. For in the liturgy God speaks to his people."

The homily is clearly kerygmatic. Vatican II emphasized "a proclamation of God's wonderful works in the history of salvation, the mystery of Christ, ever made present and active within us, especially in the celebration of the liturgy" (*Sacrosanctum Concilium* 35). The homily is beyond human words; it conveys the saving words of God. As St. Paul noted in 2 Corinthians 4:5, "For what we preach is not ourselves, but Jesus Christ as Lord, with ourselves as your servants for Jesus' sake."

The homily is familiar. Like Jesus' conversation with the two disciples on the road to Emmaus, the preacher enters into the life experience of the congregation and interjects or explains the meaning of the faith in love. The purpose here is to enlighten the mind so as to move the heart to deeper faith.

While all these dimensions of the homily need to be understood and preserved, the Church's contemporary understanding of the homily flowing from the teaching of the Second Vatican Council includes a clear catechetical dimension. In *Dei Verbum* 24 we read, "The ministry of the Word ... pastoral preaching, catechesis and all Christian instruction, in which the liturgical homily should hold the foremost place, is nourished in a healthy way and flourishes in a holy way."

Pope Paul VI, in *Evangelii Nuntiandi* 43-44, declared that the homily can certainly be a means of catechesis for the Christian community. In a world where so many Catholics have been poorly catechized, there is a clear need for the homily to be a means for deeper reflection on the meaning of faith and the teachings of the Church. Some of the great homilies of Ambrose, John Chrysostom, Augustine, Cyril, Basil, and others serve as stunning examples of how a systematic presentation of the mysteries of the faith can be expounded over the course of the liturgical year. They represent for us the coming together of the liturgical and catechetical in a profoundly transforming way.

Our purpose here is not to provide homily outlines or to impose in some artificial manner on the cycle of readings a number of catechetical themes. We believe that the homily presents a life-giving and powerful opportunity to present to the faithful — within the context of the liturgy — a complete, systematic, and comprehensive presentation of the Faith. It is a presentation, as well, that repeats itself over and over again in the course of the three-year liturgical cycle, serving to enlighten, inform, inspire, and convert mind and heart.

In a world where so many Catholics know little about their faith or have been poorly catechized, we need to seize the primary opportunity we have — the homily — as a vehicle for faith formation. The homily continues to be biblical, liturgical, kerygmatic, and familiar in nature. But in our contemporary culture, it must be catechetical as well if we are to teach our people the fullness of life in Jesus Christ and his Church.

Secondly, this book serves as an invaluable resource to those involved in the work of RCIA, sacramental, and Lectionary-based catechesis and religious education in general. There is a growing hunger among the faithful for a deeper understanding of the Scriptures and their application to daily life. Effective Lectionary-based catechesis — often used in RCIA — requires that attention be given to the complete three-year cycle of readings, with a comprehensive and complete catechesis based on the *Catechism of the Catholic Church*. This text will enable those responsible for guiding catechumens and candidates to provide effective Lectionary-based catechesis.

Lastly, this book will benefit all the faithful. From its very inception, the Church has followed the command of Jesus to "Do this in memory of me." As explained in the *Catechism of the Catholic Church*: "From that time on down to our own day the celebration of the Eucharist has been continued so that today we encounter it everywhere in the Church with the same fundamental structure. It remains the center of the Church's life" (1343).

Integral to our celebration of the Eucharist are the readings from Scripture in the Liturgy of the Word. St. Justin Martyr described for the Roman Emperor in A.D. 155 the importance of Scripture in the celebration of the Eucharist: "The memoirs of the apostles and the writings of the prophets are read, as much as time permits. When the reader has finished, he who presides over those gathered admonishes and challenges them to imitate these beautiful things."

Opening the Scriptures will enrich the homilist, the catechist, and all the faithful in their understanding of the Sacred Scriptures and the richness of the Church's teaching given to us in Jesus Christ.

REVEREND KRIS D. STUBNA, S.T.D.
Secretary for Education
Diocese of Pittsburgh

INTRODUCTION

Themes

The readings for each Sunday and feast day are listed within each cycle in **boldface**, with a brief description of the theme of each reading. Below that listing are sections from the *Catechism of the Catholic Church* that relate to those readings. The readings from each Mass are presented according to cycle A, B, or C and are identified by title and by a legend according to Sunday, season, and cycle as follows:

Legend (examples):

5La	Fifth Sunday of Lent, Cycle A
6Eb	Sixth Sunday of Easter, Cycle B
11Oa	Eleventh Sunday of Ordinary Time, Cycle A
2Aa	Second Sunday of Advent, Cycle A

An index of the themes of the *Catechism of the Catholic Church* by section correlated to the Masses of the three-year cycle is provided at the end of the book.

+ Cycle A

FIRST SUNDAY OF ADVENT (1Aa)

READING:

Isaiah 2:1-5 All nations will stream to the Lord's mountain, beating swords into plowshares. "Let us walk in the light of the Lord!"

Psalm 122 Let us go rejoicing to the house of the Lord.

Romans 13:11-14 The time is near to awake from sleep. Throw off works of darkness. Put on the Lord Jesus Christ.

Matthew 24:37-44 As in the days of Noah, stay awake and be prepared. The Son of Man comes at an hour you do not expect.

CATECHISM:

+ **668-674** Christ will come again in glory. Christ already reigns in glory and is present in history through the Church until all things are subjected to him.
+ **64-67, 758-762** The covenant unfolds. The Church — the great communion of God's people with the Trinity — is born in the Father's heart and gradually brought into being.
+ **2305, 2317** Earthly peace. The fruit of the peace of Christ. The end of warfare.

IMMACULATE CONCEPTION

READING:

Genesis 3:9-15, 20 After eating from the tree, Adam hid in fear. The woman reveals, "The serpent tricked me into it, so I ate it." God declared enmity between her offspring and the serpent's.

Psalm 98 Sing to the Lord a new song, for he has done marvelous deeds.

Ephesians 1:3-6, 11-12 God chose us before the foundation of the world to be holy and blameless.

Luke 1:26-38 The angel Gabriel announces to Mary: "Hail, full of grace!"

CATECHISM:

+ **374-379** Adam and Eve in Paradise.
+ **397-400** Original sin. Loss of holiness and harmony. Distorted image of God.
+ **489-494** Old Covenant preparations for Mary's mission. The Immaculate Conception. Espousing the divine will: "Let it be done to me."

SECOND SUNDAY OF ADVENT (2*Aa*)

READING:

Isaiah 11:1-10 A shoot from the stump of Jesse. He shall judge the poor with justice. Wolf and lamb, calf and lion. No harm or ruin on God's mountain.

Psalm 72 Justice shall flourish in his time, and fullness of peace forever.

Romans 15:4-9 May the God of endurance grant you to think in harmony. The Gentiles, too, will glorify God for his mercy.

Matthew 3:1-12 John the Baptist: "Repent, for the kingdom is at hand. I baptize with water; he will baptize with Holy Spirit and fire."

CATECHISM:

+ **50-58** God comes to meet and reveal himself to humanity. God's "Plan of Loving Goodness." Stages of revelation. The beginning up to Noah.
+ **522-524, 535-537** John, precursor of the Lord. Baptism in water and the Spirit.
+ **702** God's Spirit prepares for the time of the Messiah.

THIRD SUNDAY OF ADVENT (3Aa)

READING:

Isaiah 35:1-6, 10 The desert will bloom. "Here is your God, he comes with vindication; the blind will see, the lame will leap."

Psalm 146 Lord, come and save us.

James 5:7-10 Like the farmer, be patient. Make your hearts firm because the coming of the Lord is at hand.

Matthew 11:2-11 "Are you the one who is to come?" Jesus answered, "Tell John what you see: the blind regain sight, the lame walk. . . . None born of woman is greater than John, yet the least in the kingdom is greater than he."

CATECHISM:

+ **59-64** God chooses Abraham and forms Israel.
+ **541-550** The kingdom of God is at hand. Proclamation and signs of the kingdom.
+ **717-720** John: precursor, prophet, baptist.

FOURTH SUNDAY OF ADVENT (4Aa)

READING:

Isaiah 7:10-14 "Ask for a sign." "The virgin shall conceive, and bear a son. . . . Emmanuel."

Psalm 24 Let the Lord enter. He is king of glory.

Romans 1:1-7 Called to preach the Gospel of Christ. Descended from David, but God's own Son.

Matthew 1:18-24 Joseph's dream: "Do not be afraid. . . . It is through the Holy Spirit that this child has been conceived in Mary."

CATECHISM:

+ **430-432** The name Jesus: "God Saves." God is present in the person of his Son for our salvation.
+ **437** Born into Joseph's house (messianic lineage).
+ **484-489, 496-507, 1846** Christ is "conceived by the power of the Holy Spirit" and "born of the Virgin Mary." God's mercy revealed.
+ **51-53, 101-102, 142** God chooses to be present among us and to share his life.
+ **723-725** Role of the Holy Spirit in relation to Mary. Fulfilling the Father's plan. Manifesting the Son in her and leading us into communion.

THE NATIVITY OF THE LORD (CHRISTMAS)

READING:

Given the vast scope and great riches of the Scriptures proclaimed in the Nativity of the Lord, there is no attempt here to refer to particular passages. Instead, some overarching theological themes are offered.

CATECHISM:

✝ **456-469** Why did Word become flesh? The Incarnation. True God and True Man.

✝ **422-425** Good News. God has sent his Son, inviting people of every era to enter the joy of communion with Christ.

✝ **478** We are loved in the human heart of the Incarnate Word.

✝ **525-526** The Christmas mystery.

THE HOLY FAMILY OF JESUS, MARY, AND JOSEPH

READING:

Sirach 3:2-6, 12-14 Father and mother are to be honored.

Psalm 128 Blessed are those who fear the Lord and walk in his ways.

Colossians 3:12-21 As God's chosen ones, live in harmony and thankfulness.

Matthew 2:13-15, 19-23 The flight into Egypt.

CATECHISM:

+ **514, 530-533** The flight into Egypt. Mysteries of Jesus' hidden life (sharing human condition, family obedience, ordinary events of daily life).
+ **1655-1658** The "domestic Church."
+ **2197-2206** The nature of the family. The Christian family in God's plan.
+ **2214-2231** Duties of family members (children, Fourth Commandment, brothers/sisters, parents).

SOLEMNITY OF THE BLESSED VIRGIN MARY, MOTHER OF GOD

READING:

Numbers 6:22-27 The Lord's name was to be invoked upon the people in blessing: "The Lord bless you and keep you."

Psalm 67 May God bless us in his mercy.

Galatians 4:4-7 In the fullness of time, God sent his Son, born of a woman.

Luke 2:16-21 The shepherds went to Bethlehem and found Mary and Joseph and the infant lying in the manger. Mary reflected on all these things in her heart.

CATECHISM:

+ **422** God sent his Son.
+ **495** Mary's divine motherhood.
+ **466** Definition of "Theotokos" to clarify Christ's identity as one divine person with two true natures.
+ **527** The mystery of the circumcision.
+ **724** Through Mary, the Holy Spirit manifests the Son. Mary as burning bush of the ultimate appearance of God's presence.
+ **963-964** Mary as Mother of God and "mother of Christ's members."

EPIPHANY

READING:

Isaiah 60:1-6 Rise up in splendor. The glory of the Lord shines upon you.

Psalm 72 Lord, every nation on earth will adore you.

Ephesians 3:2-3, 5-6 The mystery made known: The Gentiles are coheirs of the promise.

Matthew 2:1-12 Magi from the East arrived. "We saw his star." Finding the child, they offered their gifts.

CATECHISM:

+ **430-440** "Jesus," "Christ": the meaning of these names.
+ **27-30** Desire for God in all human hearts, expressed in many ways.
+ **528** The mystery of Epiphany.
+ **819** Elements of sanctification are found outside the Catholic Church.
+ **2566-2567** Universal call to prayer. All religions bear witness to humanity's essential search for God. The covenant drama of human history.

BAPTISM OF THE LORD

READING:

Isaiah 42:1-4, 6-7 Here is my servant, called for the victory of justice.

Psalm 29 The Lord will bless his people with peace.

Acts 10:34-38 God shows no partiality. He proclaimed peace through Jesus Christ, beginning after John's baptism, when Jesus was anointed with the Holy Spirit.

Matthew 3:13-17 After Jesus was baptized, he saw the Spirit of God coming upon him.

CATECHISM:

+ **441-451** Jesus: Only "Son of God." Jesus as "Lord."
+ **535-537** The mystery of the baptism of Jesus.
+ **1223-1224** Christ's baptism in the economy of salvation.
+ **701, 1286** Prophetic promise that the Spirit would rest on the Messiah.

FIRST SUNDAY OF LENT (1La)

READING:

Genesis 2:7-9, 3:1-7 The creation of Adam and Eve, our first parents, and sin.

Psalm 51 Be merciful, O Lord, for we have sinned.

Romans 5:12-19 or 5:12, 17-19 Where sin increased, grace increased all the more.

Matthew 4:1-11 Fasting for forty days and forty nights, Jesus was tempted.

CATECHISM:

+ **1427-1439, 2043** Jesus calls to conversion. Interior penance and penitential practices. Church precept about fasting.
+ **396-411** Original sin. Freedom is tested. Consequences for all. God's fidelity.
+ **362, 703-704** Humanity as body and soul. God forms the world through the Son and the Spirit.
+ **374-379** Humanity in Paradise.
+ **2846-2849** "Lead us not into temptation."
+ **538-540** Temptations of Jesus.

SECOND SUNDAY OF LENT (2La)

READING:

Genesis 12:1-4 The call and commissioning of Abraham.

Psalm 33 Lord, let your mercy be on us, as we place our trust in you.

2 Timothy 1:8-10 God has saves us and calls us to a holy life.

Matthew 17:1-9 The transfigured glory of Jesus reveals that life and immortality will rob death of its power.

CATECHISM:

✝ **554-556** Transfiguration: Foretaste of the kingdom.
✝ **1450-1454** The nature of "contrition" in sacramental penance.
✝ **256** Prayer as communion with God.
✝ **2574-2577** Moses: Called through the burning bush to associate with God's compassion. Face-to-face he draws strength for intercession.
✝ **2570-2571** Prayer: Abraham's submissive heart.
✝ **2602** Jesus prays in solitude and includes all in his prayer.

THIRD SUNDAY OF LENT (3*La*)

READING:

Exodus 17:3-7 In their thirst, the Israelites grumbled. God produced water from the rock.

Psalm 95 If today you hear his voice, harden not your hearts.

Romans 5:1-2, 5-8 The life-giving presence of God has been poured into our hearts through the Holy Spirit that has been given to us.

John 4:5-42 Jesus satisfies our thirst for eternal life. Or **4:5-15, 19-26, 39, 40-42**

CATECHISM:

✝ **154-158** Faith: human search. Also God's gift.
✝ **586** Jesus: God's definitive dwelling place among people.
✝ **733-734, 1098, 2652** The liturgical assembly should accept the movement of the Spirit to prepare for the encounter with Christ. Holy Spirit as the living water.
✝ **1179** Worship in Spirit and truth.
✝ **1214-1216** Baptism as plunging into Christ. Regeneration. Enlightenment.
✝ **1217-1222** Old Testament prefiguring of baptism.
✝ **1455-1460, 2042** The role of "confession" and "satisfaction" in sacramental penance. Duty to confess serious sins (including Church precepts).
✝ **2560-2563** Prayer. Gift of God. Living water. "Heart" as center of prayer and place of covenant.
✝ **2659-2660** The "today" of prayer.

FOURTH SUNDAY OF LENT (4La)

READING:

1 Samuel 16:6-7, 10-13 The anointing of David as king. God does not see as man does.

Psalm 23 The Lord is my shepherd; there is nothing I shall want.

Ephesians 5:8-14 Through Christ, we have been called out of darkness.

John 9:1-41 (or 9:1, 6-9, 13-17, 34-38) As Jesus cures the blind man, we, too, are brought from darkness into light through the grace of baptism.

CATECHISM:

✝ **1122-1124** Sacraments presuppose and strengthen faith.

✝ **1776-1782** Judgment of conscience: recognize truth, interiority, responsibility.

✝ **1783-1785** Formation of conscience.

✝ **1786-1794** Facing choices: right and wrong judgment.

✝ **1868-1869** Structures of sin. Social sin.

✝ **2173** Jesus accused of violating the Sabbath.

✝ **2579** David's anointing in the Spirit.

FIFTH SUNDAY OF LENT (5La)

READING:

Ezekiel 37:12-14 I will open your graves. I will put my spirit in you that you may live.

Psalm 130 With the Lord there is mercy and fullness of redemption.

Romans 8:8-11 You are not in the flesh. The Spirit of the one who raised Jesus from the dead dwells in you and will give life to your mortal bodies.

John 11:1-45 or 11:3-7, 20-27, 33-45 The raising of Lazarus. "I am the resurrection and the life."

CATECHISM:

+ **402-405, 407-409** Death: the bitter fruit of sin. Christ's overthrow of death.
+ **988-1004** Resurrection of Christ and our own rising.
+ **627-628, 1214** Christ's real death. Baptism as burial with Christ.
+ **713-716** Christ's mission to bring the life-giving Spirit to those who yearn for it.
+ **2603-2604** The prayer of Christ before the raising of Lazarus.

PASSION SUNDAY

PROCESSION:

Matthew 21:1-11 Entrance to Jerusalem.

READING:

Isaiah 50:4-7 I gave my back to those who beat me. The Lord is my help. I have set my face like flint, knowing that I shall not be put to shame.

Psalm 22 My God, my God, why have you abandoned me?

Philippians 2:6-11 Christ humbled himself, obedient even to death on a cross. God greatly exalted him.

Matthew 26:14–27:66 or 27:11-54 The Passion of our Lord Jesus Christ.

CATECHISM:

+ **449** Divine title "Lord."
+ **571-572** "He was crucified under Pontius Pilate." The Paschal mystery is the heart of the Good News.
+ **606-614** Christ offers himself for sinners.
+ **713** Jesus as "servant."
+ **2605-2606** Jesus' prayer at "his hour." All human troubles are summed up in his cry from the cross.
+ **557-560** Jesus' entry into Jerusalem.

HOLY THURSDAY EVENING MASS OF THE LORD'S SUPPER

READING:

Exodus 12:1-8, 11-14 The Israelites prepared and shared the sacrificial lamb — like those who are in flight. "It is the Passover of the Lord."

Psalm 116 Our blessing-cup is a communion with the Blood of Christ.

1 Corinthians 11:23-26 As often as you eat this bread and drink the cup, you proclaim the death of the Lord until he comes.

John 13:1-15 The hour has come. Jesus loved them to the end. "I have given you a model. . . . As I have done for you, you should also do."

CATECHISM:

Glory in the cross of Christ
+ **606-607** Christ freely embraces the will of his Father.
+ **608-609** The Lamb of God loves his own to the end.
+ **610-611** At supper with his friends, Christ anticipates the free offering of his life.
+ **612** The sacrificial cup of Gethsemane.
+ **613-614** The sacrificial death of the Lamb of God.
+ **615-618** Christ's obedience even to death, loving his own to the end. Our share in his sacrifice.
+ **440, 520, 786** The "Christ," our model. His royalty is revealed in service.
+ **2746-2750** Christ's prayer when "the hour" had come.

18

The Eucharist instituted

✝ **1322-1327** The perpetuation of the sacrifice of the cross. Completes our initiation into Christ.

✝ **1334, 1337-1344** The Holy Eucharist: Rooted in the Passover event and Christ's own Passover. Done in memory of him "until he comes."

✝ **1356-1368** The Church carries out the Lord's command, offering the sacrifice of praise to the Father and the memorial of Christ's Passover.

✝ **1380-1381** The event of his Passion. Facing his departure in bodily form, Christ gives the sacrament of his true presence.

✝ **1382-1384, 1403** Eating and drinking the Paschal banquet. Awaiting its fulfillment in God's kingdom.

The Priesthood of Christ continues in his Church

✝ **1544-1545** Christ, true and only priest of the New Covenant, offers his redemptive sacrifice on the cross.

✝ **1546-1548** Christ's priesthood continues in the community of believers and, uniquely, in the ministerial priesthood.

✝ **1066-1068** The work of salvation, principally in the Paschal mystery, is manifest in the liturgy.

✝ **1085, 1088-1089** Christ is active in the liturgy, associating the Church with himself in making present his Paschal mystery.

GOOD FRIDAY
OF THE LORD'S PASSION

READING:

Isaiah 52:13–53:12 God's servant: wounded for our sins, carrying the guilt of all.

Psalm 31 Father, into your hands I commend my spirit.

Hebrews 4:14-16, 5:7-9 Jesus, the great high priest, tested in every way, yet without sin. He learned obedience from what he suffered and became the source of eternal salvation.

John 18:1–19:42 The Passion of our Lord Jesus Christ.

CATECHISM:

+ **711-716, 1505** Christ: God's servant, taking the form of a slave, yet anointed in the Spirit to bring freedom, healing, and peace to the poor.
+ **595-598** The trial of Jesus. Responsibility for his death.
+ **599-600** Christ's violent death: not outside the plan of God.
+ **601-603** Christ, the sinless one, suffers for our sins.
+ **604-605** God takes the initiative in redeeming love.
+ **1992, 2305** Justification by the cross of Christ. Christ makes peace on the cross.
+ **766** The Church is born of Christ's total self-giving, coming forth from his side as he died on the cross.

EASTER VIGIL

READING:

Given the vast scope and great riches of the Scriptures proclaimed in the Great Vigil, there is no attempt here to refer to particular passages. Instead, some overarching theological themes of this night are offered.

CATECHISM:

+ **142, 260, 460** God's fundamental purpose: The entrance of his creatures into the perfect communion of the Holy Trinity.

+ **290-301** Creation: work of the Trinity, for God's glory, upheld by God.

+ **355-361** Humanity: image of God. Restored in the New Adam.

+ **396-404, 412** Sin brings death into human history. "O happy fault."

+ **603-605, 2572** God manifests benevolent, all-embracing love as he gives his beloved Son as prefigured in the sacrifice of Isaac.

+ **624-628** Christ in the tomb. Our baptismal union with him there.

+ **272, 638, 647, 654** Resurrection: God's power in apparent powerlessness. The crowning truth of our faith. The "truly blessed night." Its meaning for us.

+ **1214-1222, 1225** Baptism: plunging into Christ's death, regeneration, and enlightenment. Rooted in history of salvation and Christ's Passover.

+ **1262, 1674** Baptism for the forgiveness of sins. A new creation. Incorporation into Christ. Union with other believers. Consecration for religious worship.

+ **1362-1364** Paschal "remembrance." Christ's Passover made present in the Eucharist.

+ **1612, 1617** Initiation into a nuptial union between God and his people.

+ **2560-2565** Prayer: Christ meets us at the well where we go in our thirst. Our covenant "from the heart." Our communion.

+ **62-64, 759-766** The formation of God's People in covenant. Expectation of renewal, gathering the scattered children — the mystery of the Church revealed from creation to the cross.

EASTER SUNDAY

READING:

Acts 10:34, 37-43 Peter preaches. In the Holy Spirit, Jesus brought goodness and healing. They put him to death, but God raised him. We who ate and drank with him after he rose from the dead are his witnesses.

Psalm 118 This is the day the Lord has made; let us rejoice and be glad.

Colossians 3:1-4 Raised with Christ, seek what is above, where Christ is. **Or 1 Corinthians 5:6-8** Clear out the old yeast that you may become fresh dough. Christ, our Paschal lamb, has been sacrificed.

John 20:1-9 Mary went to the tomb and found it empty. Peter and John then came and saw the burial cloths, for Christ had to rise from the dead. **Or (at afternoon or evening Masses) Luke 24:13-35** The road to Emmaus. They recognized him in the breaking of bread.

CATECHISM:

+ **638-642** Event of the Resurrection.
+ **647** Resurrection event transcends history.
+ **1229** Essential elements of Christian initiation.
+ **1234-1245** Mystagogy of baptismal rite.

When Luke's Emmaus Gospel is read:
+ **601** Christ's saving death was in accord with the Scriptures.
+ **1329, 1347** The Risen One reveals himself in the Eucharist.

SECOND SUNDAY OF EASTER (2*Ea*)

READING:

Acts 2:42-47 All who believed were together and had all things in common. Every day the Lord added to their number.

Psalm 118 Give thanks to the Lord for he is good. His love is everlasting.

1 Peter 1:3-9 Our merciful God has given us new birth to a living hope through the Resurrection of Jesus Christ.

John 20:19-31 The risen Lord meets with the disciples and shares the Holy Spirit. Thomas is absent and will not believe until he sees.

CATECHISM:

+ **976, 1422-1429** Sacrament of reconciliation as Easter gift.
+ **604-605, 654** God reveals his all-embracing love in the death and Resurrection of his Son.
+ **642-644** Testimonies of the Resurrection.
+ **1121** Configured to Christ: the sacramental "character."
+ **1166-1167** The "first day of the week": a day of assembly and celebration of the Resurrection.
+ **2832-2833** Newness of the kingdom is revealed in justice and sharing of material and spiritual goods ("Give us . . . our daily bread").

THIRD SUNDAY OF EASTER (3Ea)

READING:

Acts 2:14, 22-28 God worked many signs through Jesus the Nazarene. Though you crucified him, God raised him up, because it was impossible for him to be held by death.

Psalm 16 Lord, you will show us the path of life.

1 Peter 1:17-21 You were ransomed with the precious blood of Christ, the spotless lamb.

Luke 24:13-35 The Emmaus journey. They recognized him in the breaking of bread.

CATECHISM:

> ✝ **1373-1375** Christ's true presence in the Eucharist.
> ✝ **1324-1329, 1346-1347, 1362-1365, 1382-1390** The Risen One reveals himself in the Eucharist, the sacrifice and banquet in his Body and Blood.
> ✝ **642-644** Testimonies of the Resurrection.
> ✝ **109-114, 121-124** Holy Spirit: Interpreter of Scripture. Old Testament and the coming of Christ.

FOURTH SUNDAY OF EASTER (4*Ea*)

READING:

Acts 2:14, 36-41 God has made Jesus both Lord and Christ. Repent and be baptized in his name. Save yourselves from this corrupt generation.

Psalm 23 The Lord is my shepherd; there is nothing I shall want.

1 Peter 2:20-25 If you suffer for doing good, you imitate Christ, by whose wounds you have been healed. Once astray, you have returned to the shepherd and guardian of your souls.

John 10:1-10 Whoever enters through the gate is shepherd of the sheep, who calls them by name. "I am the gate. I came so they may have life, abundantly."

CATECHISM:

+ **302-308** Divine providence. Trust in Lord.
+ **754** Christ is sheepfold and gateway to God.
+ **1465** Presence and ministry of the Good Shepherd.
+ **197, 1226-1228, 1246-1255** Proclaiming the creed. Baptism in the Church. Adults, children, and faith.
+ **1267-1271** Baptism makes us members of Christ's Body, united also with each other.
+ **2156-2159** The baptismal name. God calls us by name.

FIFTH SUNDAY OF EASTER (5Ea)

READING:

Acts 6:1-7 The Church continues to grow. The twelve select seven Spirit-filled men to serve at the table.

Psalm 33 Lord, let your mercy be on us, as we place our trust in you.

1 Peter 2:4-9 Come to Christ, the cornerstone. You are a chosen race, a royal priesthood.

John 14:1-12 Many dwellings in my Father's house. I am the way, the truth, and the life.

CATECHISM:

+ **516** Christ's mysteries manifest God's love.
+ **897-900** Lay faithful are called to transform the temporal order.
+ **901, 1121** All the faithful participate in Christ's priestly office.
+ **909-913** Lay persons participate in Christ's kingly office.
+ **1179** Assembly of the faithful as living stones of the spiritual house.
+ **1268** Baptism and sharing in priesthood of Jesus.
+ **1140-1144** Whole community celebrates.
+ **2466-2470** He is the Truth.

SIXTH SUNDAY OF EASTER (6*Ea*)

READING:

Acts 8:5-8, 14-17 Philip proclaimed Christ and baptized in Samaria. Peter and John went there and laid hands upon them, and they received the Holy Spirit.

Psalm 66 Let all the earth cry out to God with joy.

1 Peter 3:15-18 Be ready to explain your hope. If necessary, bear suffering like Christ who, dead in the flesh, came to life in the Spirit.

John 14:15-21 Love me. Keep my commandments. The Father will send another Advocate. I will not leave you orphans.

CATECHISM:

+ **1066-1075** Celebration of Christian faith in liturgy.
+ **1286-1289, 1293-1296, 1300** Confirmation. Apostolic practice. The essential rite of the sacrament.
+ **1302-1314** Effects of confirmation. Its recipient and minister.
+ **2615** In the Holy Spirit, Christian prayer is communion of love.
+ **729** Promise of the Spirit of Truth.

SOLEMNITY OF THE ASCENSION OF THE LORD

READING:

Acts 1:1-11 After appearing to them through forty days, the risen Christ was lifted up. They were to await the baptism with the Holy Spirit.

Psalm 47 God mounts his throne to shouts of joy. A blare of trumpets for the Lord.

Ephesians 1:17-23 May God's power work in you. The power that raised Christ from the dead, seated him at God's right hand, and placed all things under his feet.

Matthew 28:16-20 "All power has been given to me. Go and make disciples of all nations. I am with you."

CATECHISM:

+ **659-664** Ascension into Heaven, sits at right hand.
+ **830-831, 849-851, 858** The Church's "catholic" and "apostolic" mission.
+ **1120-1122** Ordained ministry at service of the baptismal priesthood. Mission to evangelize.

SEVENTH SUNDAY OF EASTER (7Ea)

READING:

Acts 1:12-14 After the Lord's ascension, the disciples devoted themselves to prayer.

Psalm 27 I believe that I shall see the good things of the Lord in the land of the living.

1 Peter 4:13-16 If you are insulted for the name of Christ, blessed are you, but let no one do evil.

John 17:1-11 "The hour has come. Father, glorify your Son. I pray for those you gave me; they are in the world as I come to you."

CATECHISM:

+ **1-3** Essence of human life: to know and love God.
+ **1136-1144** Heavenly liturgy and liturgy on earth.
+ **2746-2751** Christ's "priestly prayer."
+ **1099-1109** Holy Spirit and Christ in the liturgy.
+ **2142-2149, 2807-2815** Hallowing the name of God.

PENTECOST

VIGIL (CATECHISM):

2655-2658 Prayer: internalizes the liturgy and relies on faith, hope, and love.

READING:

Acts 2:1-11 They were all filled with the Holy Spirit and began to speak. All who heard them heard in their native language.

Psalm 104 Lord, send out your Spirit, and renew the face of the earth.

1 Corinthians 12:3-7, 12-13 Different gifts, but the same Spirit. In one Spirit we were all baptized into one body, able to say "Jesus is Lord."

John 20:19-23 The risen Jesus meets his disciples: "Peace be with you. As the Father has sent me, I send you. Receive the Holy Spirit. Whose sins you forgive are forgiven them."

CATECHISM:

+ **152, 683-686** Who is the Holy Spirit?
+ **731-732** The Pentecost: Christ's Passover fulfilled and the Holy Trinity fully revealed.
+ **1087, 1120** "Apostolic succession" as entrusting the Holy Spirit by Christ to the apostles and successors.
+ **1287-1288** All the baptized share the messianic character of Christ.
+ **781-786** The Church in the Spirit: priestly, prophetic, royal People of God.
+ **976** Christ gives the Spirit for forgiveness of sin.

SOLEMNITY OF THE MOST HOLY TRINITY

READING:

Exodus 34:4-6, 8-9 Moses receives God's name, "The Lord, the Lord, a merciful and gracious God."

(Psalm) Daniel 3:20-23 Glory and praise forever!

2 Corinthians 13:11-13 Live in peace, in the grace of Christ. The love of God. The fellowship of the Holy Spirit.

John 3:16-18 God so loved the world that he sent his Son so the world might be saved through him.

CATECHISM:

+ **249-256** Holy Trinity: formation of Church's dogma.
+ **210-211** "I Am" — God's gracious mercy.
+ **232-237** Holy Trinity: Central mystery of faith.
+ **1083, 2627, 2793** Our prayer to the Father, whose boundless love comes in Christ through the Spirit.

SOLEMNITY OF THE MOST HOLY BODY AND BLOOD OF CHRIST

READING:

Deuteronomy 8:2-3, 14-16 Do not forget the Lord, who brought you out of Egypt and fed you in your hunger with food unknown to your fathers.

Psalm 147 Praise the Lord, Jerusalem.

1 Corinthians 10:16-17 The cup of blessing, the bread we break. Participation in Christ's Blood and Body. The loaf is one. We are one body.

John 6:51-58 I am the living bread from heaven. My flesh and blood are true food and drink. Eat and live forever.

CATECHISM:

+ **1382-1401** Communion with Christ. Disposition. Unity of the Body of Christ. Fruits of communion.
+ **1333-1334** Eucharist: "Passover bread" and "cup of blessing."
+ **1524, 2835-2837** Bread of Life as "viaticum" and "daily bread."
+ **1200-1206** Celebration of the liturgical mystery through the ages: unity in diversity.

SECOND SUNDAY OF ORDINARY TIME (20a)

READING:

Isaiah 49:3, 5-6 I will make you a light to the nations in order that my salvation reaches to the ends of the earth.

Psalm 40 Here am I, Lord. I come to do your will.

1 Corinthians 1:1-3 Through Christ you have been called to be holy.

John 1:29-34 Jesus is the Lamb of God who takes away the sins of the world.

CATECHISM:

+ **717-720, 727-730** Jesus: Anointed in the Holy Spirit.
+ **713** "Servant Song": Jesus gives the Holy Spirit not as outsider but as servant.
+ **64** The New Covenant is for all.
+ **408** The "sin of the world."
+ **486** The Son is anointed by the Spirit from the beginning of his human existence.
+ **523, 608** The "Lamb who takes away the sin of the world."
+ **689-690** The joint mission of the Son and the Spirit.

THIRD SUNDAY OF ORDINARY TIME (30a)

READING:

Isaiah 8:22–9:3 The people have seen a great light.

Psalm 27 The Lord is my light and my salvation.

1 Corinthians 1:10-13, 17 In Christ, all are called to be united, one in the Lord.

Matthew 4:12-23 or 4:12-17 In order to fulfill what was said through Isaiah, Jesus went to Capernaum.

CATECHISM:

+ **1989** The first grace of the Spirit is conversion.
+ **813-816** Church is one because its source is one. Its unity is expressed in charity, profession of one faith, worship and apostolic succession.

For Week of Prayer for Christian Unity:
+ **817-819** Wounds to ecumenical unity.
+ **820-822** Toward unity. Christ's gift, renewal activities, conversion of heart, and common prayer. It is the concern of all.
+ **858-860** The apostles' mission.
+ **877-878** The call to ministry: a service exercised personally yet in collegial solidarity.

FOURTH SUNDAY OF
ORDINARY TIME (40*a*)

READING:

Zephaniah 2:3, 3:12-13 Blest are the humble of the earth.

Psalm 146

1 Corinthians 1:26-31 God has chosen the weak of the world to confound the wise.

Matthew 5:1-12 Blessed are the poor in spirit. The kingdom of heaven is theirs!

CATECHISM:

+ **272** God's apparent powerlessness and foolishness.
+ **2444-2445** Church's love for the poor.
+ **408** The "sin of the world."
+ **711, 716** The "remnant." The humble and meek welcome Christ.
+ **520-521** Jesus as a model of humility and poverty. Live in him.
+ **1716-1724** The beatitudes.
+ **544** The kingdom belongs to the poor, lowly, little ones.
+ **2544-2548** Poverty of heart, spirit of detachment.
+ **2305** Peace of Christ: Blessed are the peacemakers.
+ **2816-2821** God's people yearn and pray. "Thy kingdom come!"

FIFTH SUNDAY OF
ORDINARY TIME (50a)

READING:

Isaiah 58:7-10 Your light will shine like the dawn.

Psalm 112 The just man is a light in darkness to the upright.

1 Corinthians 2:1-5 The mystery of Christ crucified has been announced to you.

Matthew 5:13-16 You are the light of the world.

CATECHISM:

+ **2446-2449** Care for the poor. Works of mercy.
+ **2475-2479** Offenses against the truth of another (false witness, rash judgment).
+ **782** Characteristics of people of God. Mission as "salt of the earth."
+ **1243** In Christ, the newly baptized become the light of the world.
+ **774-775** Church as sacrament of salvation (sign and instrument).
+ **153-156** Faith as grace and as human act.
+ **164-165** Walk by faith, not sight. Experiences of evil and suffering can shake faith, but look to Jesus.
+ **1741** The Holy Cross as salvation and liberation.

SIXTH SUNDAY OF ORDINARY TIME (6Oa)

READING:

Sirach 15:15-20 Life and death, good and evil — you can choose.

Psalm 119 Blessed are they who follow the law of the Lord!

1 Corinthians 2:6-10 God's mysterious wisdom: "Eye has not seen."

Matthew 5:17-37 "I have come to fulfill the law; you have heard it said... but I say..."

CATECHISM:

+ **221** God's innermost secret. Our destiny to share the exchange of love that is God.
+ **1024-1027** Heaven: The perfect communion with God beyond our imagining.
+ **1721-1724** Christian "beatitude." To know, love, serve God, and enter Paradise. We are confronted with decisive choices as we purify our hearts and seek greatest blessedness.
+ **577-581, 707-708** Jesus and the Law.
+ **1967-1968** Gospel fulfills Law, proceeding from reform of the heart.
+ **2032-2034** Church as teacher.
+ **2054** Jesus revealed the Spirit working in the letter of the Law.
+ **2064-2073** The Commandments in Church tradition.

+ **2608, 2838** True prayer ("gift to the altar") is rooted in conversion ("go first"). "Forgive us ... as we forgive."
+ **2466** To follow Jesus is to live in the truth (simply "yes" or "no").
+ **2258-2262** Respect for human life (Fifth Commandment).

SEVENTH SUNDAY OF ORDINARY TIME (7Oa)

READING:

Leviticus 19:1-2, 17-18 Be holy. Take no revenge. Love neighbor as yourself.

Psalm 103 The Lord is kind and merciful.

1 Corinthians 3:16-23 You are temples of God, holy. You belong to Christ.

Matthew 5:38-48 Do not resist evil. Turn the other cheek, love your enemies. Be perfect as your heavenly Father is perfect.

CATECHISM:

+ **823-827** The Church: endowed with holiness, yet still in need of purification.
+ **2013-2015** Universal call to holiness. Cross as path to perfection.
+ **1997-1999** Grace: participation in life of God. Thus we can call God "Father." Grace sanctifies or "deifies" human beings.
+ **1931-1933** Look on all as neighbor, even enemies.
+ **1693, 1825, 2262-2267, 2302-2303** Imitate Christ, who loved us while we were his enemies. No hatred or vengeance. The challenge of legitimate defense (Fifth Commandment).
+ **2844** Prayer: Share in God's compassion, even for our enemies.

EIGHTH SUNDAY OF
ORDINARY TIME (8Oa)

READING:

Isaiah 49:14-15 Can a mother forget her child? I will never forget you.

Psalm 62 Rest in God alone, my soul.

1 Corinthians 4:1-5 Paul is servant of Christ, steward of God's mysteries. The Lord alone will judge.

Matthew 6:24-34 No serving two masters. Do not worry. Look at the birds and the flowers.

CATECHISM:

+ **301, 305** God does not abandon his creatures. He upholds them. Jesus calls us to trust this divine providence.
+ **2113** Avoid "idolatry" that divinizes what is not God.
+ **2547, 2830** Poverty of heart. Trusting in God frees from anxiety.
+ **2729** Prayer: Avoiding distraction in our relationship with God by returning to our hearts.
+ **2632, 2659** Prayer centers on the search for the kingdom in the "today" where the Father's providence is found.
+ **859** Apostolic mission. Being stewards of God's mysteries.
+ **914-919, 925-927** The consecrated life. Seeking first the kingdom.

NINTH SUNDAY OF
ORDINARY TIME (90a)

READING:

Deuteronomy 11:18, 26-28, 32 Write these words on your heart. Observe them.

Psalm 31 Lord, be my rock of safety.

Romans 3:21-25, 28 Righteousness has been revealed apart from the Law. A person is justified by faith

Matthew 7:21-27 The house on rock, the house on sand. Act on God's words.

CATECHISM:

+ **398-399** Sin robs humanity of divinizing glory and original holiness.
+ **402-405** Adam's sin affects everyone.
+ **1963-1965** Old Law: holy and good, but imperfect. A preparation for the Gospel, as prophets foresaw.
+ **433** Christ's blood as "expiation."
+ **1987-2005** "Justification": merited by Christ, offered by grace. We cooperate with it through faith.
+ **1970** The Gospel requires that we put God's words into practice.
+ **2150-2155** Calling on the name of the Lord in vain.
+ **2611, 2794-2796** Prayer: not words but disposing the heart to do the will of the Father "in heaven."
+ **2809** The "glory of God."

TENTH SUNDAY OF
ORDINARY TIME (10*0a*)

READING:

Hosea 6:3-6 I desire love, not sacrifice.

Psalm 50 To the upright I will show the saving power of God.

Romans 4:18-25 Abraham believed. His faith was credited to him as righteousness.

Matthew 9:9-13 The call of Matthew. Jesus eats with sinners.

CATECHISM:

+ **545, 589** Jesus invites sinners to the table of the kingdom. His mercy scandalized the Pharisees.
+ **1443** Christ's forgiveness reintegrates sinners into the People of God. The sign: He ate with sinners.
+ **2100** The acceptable sacrifice. A broken spirit.
+ **144-146, 1819, 2000-2002** Abraham's faith. His hope.
+ **654, 977** Christ was raised for our justification.
+ **1991** Justification: acceptance of God's righteousness through faith in Christ.
+ **2655-2660** Wellsprings of prayer: the liturgy. Our faith, hope, and love. Our awareness of "today."

ELEVENTH SUNDAY OF ORDINARY TIME (11*Oa*)

READING:

Exodus 19:2-6 On eagle's wings I brought you to myself to be a kingdom of priests, a holy nation.

Psalm 100 We are his people, the sheep of his flock.

Romans 5:6-11 While we were sinners, Christ died for us. We are saved by his life.

Matthew 9:36-10:8 The harvest is abundant. He sent them out to cure illness.

CATECHISM:

+ **604, 1825** God takes the initiative in benevolent love, even for enemies.
+ **761-762, 2810** Church prefigured in the Old Covenant. Gathering of a holy nation.
+ **1141** The liturgical assembly. A holy priesthood.
+ **3, 543-544, 849-856, 863-865, 1501-1507** God's love is the foundation of missionary outreach to everyone to enter the kingdom of God. The Christian vocation is apostolic.

TWELFTH SUNDAY OF
ORDINARY TIME (12Oa)

READING:

Jeremiah 20:10-13 Terror is all around, but God who rescues the poor is with me.

Psalm 69 Lord, in your great love, answer me.

Romans 5:12-15 Sin and death enter the world through Adam. From Christ comes grace.

Matthew 10-26-33 Do not fear those who can kill the body. Yet the God who can destroy all is full of care.

CATECHISM:

+ **399-403** Adam's sin has consequences for all.
+ **602-605** Christ's gracious gift of mercy is for all.
+ **1008-1009** Death, a consequence of sin, is transformed by Christ.
+ **362-368** "Soul": our innermost aspect. "Heart": where we decide for or against God.
+ **1033-1037** Hell (Gehenna) and the call to responsible use of freedom.
+ **303, 305** Trust in God's providence.
+ **1816** Call to acknowledge Christ before others.

THIRTEENTH SUNDAY OF ORDINARY TIME (13*Oa*)

READING:

2 Kings 4:8-11, 14-16 The Suhunemite woman offers hospitality to the holy man Elisha. He promises that she and her husband will have a son.

Psalm 89 Forever I will sing the goodness of the Lord.

Romans 6:3-4, 8-11 In baptism we enter Christ's death, so that, rising with him, we may live a new life.

Matthew 10:37-42 Love nothing more than Christ. Take the cross. Anyone who welcomes you welcomes me.

CATECHISM:

+ **537, 628, 654, 790, 1212-1213, 1220, 1226-1228** Baptism joins us to Christ's body and plunges us into his death and Resurrection.
+ **618, 2232-2233** Following Christ means bearing his cross. This vocation surpasses even family ties.
+ **858** The apostolic mission continues that of Christ.

FOURTEENTH SUNDAY OF
ORDINARY TIME (140a)

READING:

Zechariah 9:9-10 Zion, rejoice. See your savior meekly riding an ass. He will banish horse and chariot and proclaim peace.

Psalm 145 I will praise your name forever, my king and my God.

Romans 8:9 11-13 You are in the spirit, not the flesh. Raised with Christ. Put to death the evil deeds of the body.

Matthew 11:25-30 What is hidden from the learned is revealed to merest children. Come to me, I will refresh you. I am gentle and humble of heart.

CATECHISM:

✝ **238-240** How the Son speaks of the Father.
✝ **989-990** The Resurrection of the body. "Flesh" as our weakened, mortal state.
✝ **459, 559** Jesus, our model of holiness, enters Jerusalem and "conquers" not by force but by humility and truth.
✝ **1503-1505** Christ, the compassionate one, takes the weight of the world on his shoulders.
✝ **544, 2603, 2779, 2784-2785** Jesus prays in thanksgiving for the Father's gracious plan. We must pray with a childlike confidence.
✝ **153-156** Faith as gift of God and human act.

FIFTEENTH SUNDAY OF ORDINARY TIME (15Oa)

READING:

Isaiah 55:10-11 Like the life-nourishing rain, God's Word is effective.

Psalm 65 The seed that falls on good ground will yield a fruitful harvest.

Romans 8:18-23 All creation is waiting, even groaning, to see the revelation of God's freeing and life-giving redemption.

Matthew 13:1-23 (or 1-9) The farmer sowed the seed. It fell on different kinds of ground.

CATECHISM:

+ **399-400, 1042, 1046-1047, 1741** Creation's bondage. Liberation of humanity and the destiny of the cosmos.
+ **2630** Creation's prayer as "groaning."
+ **546** Notion of "parable."
+ **101-102, 291** The Word of God: perfect in Christ.
+ **1703-1709** Human vocation to respond to voice of God by doing good and avoiding evil.
+ **2652-2654** God's Word: wellspring for prayer.

SIXTEENTH SUNDAY OF ORDINARY TIME (16*0a*)

READING:

Wisdom 12:13, 16-19 God the mighty cares for all, governs with leniency, and allows repentance for sins.

Psalm 86 Lord, you are good and forgiving.

Romans 8:26-27 The Spirit helps us in weakness and intercedes for us in groans that cannot be put in words.

Matthew 13:24-43 (or 24-30) Good seed was sown, but weeds appeared. Let them grow together. The mustard seed. The yeast in the woman's loaf.

CATECHISM:

+ **2630, 2634** Our signs of petition. Intercessory prayer.
+ **2615, 2652, 2559, 2629-2630, 2672, 2736, 2766** Prayer in the Holy Spirit. The "living water" in our hearts. Our helper in prayer.
+ **827** The Church: Weeds of sin mixed with wheat of Gospel.
+ **386-387** Sin present in human history.
+ **309-311** How does evil exist? Providence and the scandal of evil.

SEVENTEENTH SUNDAY OF ORDINARY TIME (17Oa)

READING:

1 Kings 3:5, 7-12 God grants the prayer of Solomon for an understanding heart to judge the people.

Psalm 119 Lord, I love your commands.

Romans 8:28-30 God makes all things work for the good. Calling us to share the image of his Son and justifying us.

Matthew 13:44-52 (or 44-46) The buried treasure. The fine pearl. The dragnet cast into the sea.

CATECHISM:

+ **1776-1777, 1780, 1806** Conscience: Place for discerning God's call to judge prudently and to act.
+ **311-314, 1817, 1820-1821** Hope in providence, even under trial.
+ **257, 2012-2013** Our destiny to be God's children. Call to holiness through union with Christ.
+ **1034-1035** Fate of the wicked: the fiery furnace.
+ **328-333** Angels: centered on Christ and sent to do his work.

EIGHTEENTH SUNDAY OF ORDINARY TIME (18Oa)

READING:

Isaiah 55:1-3 All you thirsty, come to the water. Do not waste money on what will not satisfy. Come to me. I will renew the everlasting covenant.

Psalm 145 The hand of the Lord feeds us. He answers all our needs.

Romans 8:35, 37-39 Nothing can separate us from God's love in Christ.

Matthew 14:13-21 Jesus took the five loaves and two fish, blessed and broke them, and fed the crowd — with twelve baskets left over.

CATECHISM:

+ **2560-2561** Prayer: the encounter of God's thirst with ours.
+ **2652-2654** Reading of Scripture as a wellspring of prayer.
+ **395** Power of Satan is not infinite and cannot overcome providence or prevent the building up of God's reign.
+ **1006-1009** Death: the last enemy to be destroyed.
+ **301, 2086** God sustains creation and is almighty and beneficent. Who could not place all hope in him?
+ **1333-1335, 1365** Eucharist: food taken up and shared. The New Covenant in Christ's blood.
+ **2828-2831, 2835, 2837** Need and prayer for "our daily bread."

NINETEENTH SUNDAY OF ORDINARY TIME (19Oa)

READING:

1 Kings 19:9, 11-13 Elijah found the Lord God not in a strong, heavy wind but in a tiny whispering sound.

Psalm 85 Lord, let us see your kindness, and grant us your salvation.

Romans 9:1-5 For the sake of the Israelites — with their heritage as God's people — I could even wish to be separated from Christ.

Matthew 14:22-33 The disciples, tossed in the waves, see Jesus. He tells Peter to come to him across the water.

CATECHISM:

+ **839-840** The irrevocable call of the Jewish people.
+ **142-143** Faith: response to God's revelation and invitation to join him.
+ **156-157** Faith: its reliance on God's truth and its certainty.
+ **441-442, 448-450** Jesus' titles. "Son of God": the only "Lord" we should submit to.
+ **2583** Elijah's encounter with God: Letting God lead our heart to where he can be found (prayer).

TWENTIETH SUNDAY OF
ORDINARY TIME (20Oa)

READING:

Isaiah 56:1, 6-7 Observe what is right. I will bring the righteous to my holy mountain, to joy in my house of prayer for all.

Psalm 67 O God, let all the nations praise you!

Romans 11:13-15, 29-32 The return of Israel will mean life from the dead. God's gift and call are irrevocable.

Matthew 15:21-28 The Canaanite woman's great faith: "Have pity on me.... Even dogs get the leavings from their masters' tables."

CATECHISM:

+ **674, 839** The Messiah's glorious return is bound up with Israel's inclusion, because Israel's call is irrevocable.
+ **439** Jesus is recognized even by some Gentiles as Messiah.
+ **543-544** The kingdom, first announced to Israel, is meant for all.
+ **2610** Filial boldness: a characteristic of Jesus' way of prayer.
+ **2567** All are called to encounter God in prayer.
+ **161, 1504-1505** The sick seek Jesus. He calls for faith so they can receive the gift of salvation.

TWENTY-FIRST SUNDAY OF ORDINARY TIME (21*Oa*)

READING:

Isaiah 22:15, 19-23 I will take your authority and give it to another. I place the key of the House of David on his shoulder.

Psalm 138 Lord, your love is eternal.

Romans 11:33-36 The depth of God's wisdom. From him, through him, and for him all things are.

Matthew 16:13-20 Who do you say I am? "You are the Messiah." And Jesus replied, "You are the rock; I will give you the keys to the kingdom of heaven."

CATECHISM:

+ **424, 153** Profession of faith in Jesus is the rock on which the Church is built. Faith as divine gift.
+ **436, 41-42** Peter's use of the titles "Messiah," "Son of God."
+ **551-553** Peter and the "keys of the kingdom."
+ **857, 880-887** Church is founded on the apostles. The office of Peter in the college of bishops.
+ **2500-2502** God's beauty is revealed in the language of creation. His Word, his wisdom. Sacred art is the glorification of the truthful and beautiful God.

TWENTY-SECOND SUNDAY OF ORDINARY TIME (22*Oa*)

READING:

Jeremiah 20:1-9 "You duped me." The Word of the Lord brought me derision, but I could not hold it in.

Psalm 63 My soul is thirsting for you, O Lord my God.

Romans 12:1-2 Offer your bodies as a living sacrifice. Do not conform to this age but be transformed.

Matthew 16:21-27 Jesus indicated that he must suffer. Peter judges by human standards. Following Jesus entails taking up the cross and losing ourselves for his sake.

CATECHISM:

> ✝ **2584** Prophetic prayer is sometimes complaint.
> ✝ **1691-1696** Christians are rescued from darkness and called to walk the moral road to life, not death.
> ✝ **2030-2031** Moral life is spiritual worship.
> ✝ **554-555** To enter his glory, Jesus must go by way of the cross.
> ✝ **607, 609** In his suffering Jesus freely embraces the Father's plan of redeeming love.
> ✝ **618** We are called to become partners in Christ's Paschal mystery, carrying the cross.
> ✝ **363** Soul: our innermost self.
> ✝ **678-679** Christ in glory as the Judge.

TWENTY-THIRD SUNDAY OF ORDINARY TIME (23Oa)

READING:

Ezekiel 33:7-9 You are a watchman for Israel. You must warn the wicked.

Psalm 95 If today you hear his voice, harden not your heart.

Romans 13:8-10 Love is the fulfillment of the law.

Matthew 18:15-20 If your brother sins, go to him. If he listens, you have won him over. Where two or three are gathered in my name, I am there.

CATECHISM:

+ **2055** The twofold commandment of love.
+ **553, 1444-1445, 2032-2040** The Church's teaching authority. "Binding and loosing" in reconciliation.
+ **1088** In the Church's liturgy, Christ is in our midst.
+ **1826-1829** Charity: the greatest of virtues. Includes fraternal correction.
+ **2044-2046** The witness value of a good Christian life.
+ **2447** In works of mercy we come to the spiritual and bodily aid of our neighbor.

TWENTY-FOURTH SUNDAY OF ORDINARY TIME (24Oa)

READING:

Sirach 27:30–28:7 Forgive injustice. Do not refuse mercy. Then, when you pray, your own sins will be forgiven.

Psalm 103 The Lord is kind and merciful. Slow to anger and rich in compassion.

Romans 14:7-9 We are not our own masters. We belong to the Lord.

Matthew 18:21-35 Forgive "seventy times seven times." Do not act like the unforgiving servant but like the merciful master.

CATECHISM:

+ **953** We belong to one another in the charity of the communion of saints.
+ **981-983** Christ entrusts the Church with the ministry of reconciliation. No offense is beyond forgiveness.
+ **1010-1014** To die as the Lord's servants.
+ **2838-2845** Lord's prayer: "Forgive us... as we forgive."

TWENTY-FIFTH SUNDAY OF ORDINARY TIME (25Oa)

READING:

Isaiah 55:6-9 Seek the Lord. Forsake wickedness. God's thoughts are not our thoughts.

Psalm 145 The Lord is near to all who call upon him.

Philippians 1:20-24, 27 To me, life is Christ. I want to be with Christ, but I also want to work productively on earth.

Matthew 20:1-16 Throughout the day, the owner hired workers for the vineyard — and paid all the daily wage. "Are you envious because I am generous?" The last shall be first.

CATECHISM:

+ **1010-1013** In Christ, death is gain.
+ **40-52, 210-211** Our efforts to speak about the "inexpressible" God — but also God's revelation of himself in loving goodness.
+ **588-589** The scandal of Jesus' mercy.
+ **543-546** The kingdom of God is for all.
+ **2429-2436** Justice in matters of employment and wages.

TWENTY-SIXTH SUNDAY OF ORDINARY TIME (260a)

READING:

Ezekiel 18:25-28 You say, "The Lord's way is not fair." But when the sinner turns away from wickedness, he shall live.

Psalm 125 Remember your mercies, O Lord.

Philippians 2:1-11 (or 1-5) Have the same attitude as Christ, who emptied himself and took the form of a slave.

Matthew 21:28-32 The man asked his sons, "Go, work in the field." One said "Yes," the other said, "No" — but only the second son actually went. Tax collectors and prostitutes are entering the kingdom before the unrepentant.

CATECHISM:

+ **457-466, 602-603, 608-609, 616** To serve and save us, Christ takes on our condition, even unto death on the cross.
+ **908, 2842, 2635** With the "mind of Christ" we seek unity and forgiveness and look to the interests of others.
+ **535, 541-545** John the Baptist's ministry prepares for Jesus' call to repentance.
+ **587-591** Jesus and Israel's faith in God as Savior. Repentant sinners accept him, but some leaders find him a scandal.

TWENTY-SEVENTH SUNDAY OF ORDINARY TIME (27Oa)

READING:

Isaiah 5:1-7 My friend cared for his vineyard, but it produced wild grapes. The vineyard of the Lord is the house of Israel.

Psalm 80 The vineyard of the Lord is the house of Israel.

Philippians 4:6-9 Present your needs to God, whose peace is beyond understanding. Be directed to all that is true, honest, virtuous.

Matthew 21:33-43 The tenant farmers killed even the vineyard owner's son. The owner will punish them and give the vineyard to others who will produce fruit. The rejected stone becomes the keystone.

CATECHISM:

+ **2633** Every need can be a motive for prayer.
+ **1803-1809, 1830-1832** Human virtues. The "gifts" and "fruits" of the Spirit.
+ **755** Church as "vineyard."
+ **529-530** Revealed already in the Christmas mysteries, Christ is the Beloved Son who will be rejected.
+ **1850-1851** Sin as opposition to God.
+ **2258-2262, 2268-2269** Sacredness of life. Humanity's murderous violence.
+ **2705-2708** Meditative prayer.

TWENTY-EIGHTH SUNDAY OF ORDINARY TIME (28Oa)

READING:

Isaiah 25:6-10 On this mountain, the Lord will prepare a feast for all peoples. He will destroy death and wipe away tears. "Behold our God to whom we looked to save us."

Psalm 23 I shall live in the house of the Lord all the days of my life.

Philippians 4:12-14, 19-20 I have learned how to cope. In him who is my strength, I have strength for everything.

Matthew 22:1-14 (or 1-10) Those invited to the wedding banquet refused to come. So the king sent servants to gather anyone they found. But one without a wedding garment was cast outside.

CATECHISM:

+ **272-274** God's power in apparent powerlessness.
+ **2339-2340** Personal integrity. Self-mastery and ascesis adapted to situations.
+ **2742-2743** Prayer as humble, persevering love.
+ **543-546, 796** Jesus invites all (even sinners) to the kingdom's table (the wedding feast of Christ and his bride) — but this requires a choice.
+ **1243-1244** Christian initiation: The newly baptized (now God's child and clothed in the wedding garment) comes to the marriage supper of the Lamb.
+ **1335, 1382, 1385** Eucharist: banquet of intimate union (for which one must prepare).

TWENTY-NINTH SUNDAY OF ORDINARY TIME (29Oa)

READING:

Isaiah 45:1, 4-6 The Lord said to Cyrus, "It is I who arm you, though you know me not. I am the Lord, there is no other."

Psalm 96 Give the Lord glory and honor.

1 Thessalonians 1:1-5 We thank God as we remember your faith, love, and hope. Our preaching was not a matter of mere words, but of power.

Matthew 22:15-21 Repay to Caesar what belongs to Caesar and to God what belongs to God.

CATECHISM:

+ **75, 860** Apostolic call to preach the Gospel to communicate the gifts of God to all, the source of life for all ages.
+ **303-308** God, the sovereign master of history, works through creatures to manifest providence.
+ **1897-1904, 2235-2237, 2242** Duties of civil authorities and of citizens toward them.
+ **450, 2113** Only Christ is Lord, to whom we make ultimate submission. "Idolatry" of state when treated as ultimate.
+ **2471-2474** Jesus: witness to the truth.

THIRTIETH SUNDAY OF
ORDINARY TIME (30Oa)

READING:

Exodus 22:20-26 Do not oppress the alien, or harm the widow or orphan. I hear the poor. I am compassionate.

Psalm 18 I love you, Lord ,my strength.

1 Thessalonians 1:5-10 Like us, you received the Word with joy and turned to God from idols to await the return of his Son.

Matthew 22:34-40 "Which commandment is the greatest?" "Love God ... and your neighbor."

CATECHISM:

+ **2054-2055** Christ: The Ten Commandments summed up in the "two great commandments."
+ **218-221, 2061-2063** First, God loves us: The commandments express the divine-human covenant and are secondary to it.
+ **356-357, 368, 2563** Human beings are created for the covenant of love, rooted in the "heart."
+ **1968** Gospel's law fulfills rather than diminishes the commandments, through imitation of the divine perfection of generosity.

THIRTY-FIRST SUNDAY OF
ORDINARY TIME (31*Oa*)

READING:

Malachi 1:14-2:2, 8-10 You have strayed from the way and caused others to stumble by your teaching. But is there not just one God and Father?

Psalm 131 In you, Lord, I have found my peace.

1 Thessalonians 2:7-9, 13 We were gentle with you as a nursing mother, wanting to share with you the tidings and ourselves. That message is God's Word at work in you.

Matthew 23:1-12 Scribes and Pharisees. They do not practice what they preach. They act to be noticed. Avoid titles such as rabbi and teacher. Whoever exalts himself will be humbled.

CATECHISM:

+ **131-132** Scripture as basic nourishment in the life of the Church.
+ **238-240, 2786-2793** God as "Father." Prayer to "Our" Father.
+ **436, 578-581** Jesus as "messiah" and "rabbi." His relationship with the Pharisees.
+ **520, 559** Jesus as model for all disciples. He humbles himself, even as a "king."
+ **871-873, 876** Ministry of Church continues the office of Christ as teacher, priest, pastor. Its character as service.
+ **888-892** The Magisterium: exercising the care of Christ the Teacher.

THIRTY-SECOND SUNDAY OF ORDINARY TIME (32Oa)

READING:

Wisdom 6:12-16 Wisdom is resplendent and readily perceived by those who love her. She meets and favors those who keep vigil for her.

Psalm 63 My soul is thirsting for you, O Lord my God.

1 Thessalonians 4:13-18 (or 13-14) Do not yield to grief like the hopeless, for God will raise with Jesus those who have fallen asleep in him. Then the living will be gathered to be always with the Lord.

Matthew 25:1-13 The wise and the foolish virgins take their lamps to keep watch for the bridegroom. When he came, those who were ready went into the feast with him. Stay awake. You know neither the day nor the hour.

CATECHISM:

+ **988-991, 1001, 1005-1014** Looking toward the resurrection of the dead. Life is changed, not ended.
+ **1030-1032** Final purification of those who die in God's friendship but are still imperfect (purgatory).
+ **671-672, 1048, 2612** Knowing not the time, we wait and watch for Christ's coming in glory. The watchfulness of prayer.
+ **769, 796** Church made glorious in heaven, united with Christ her bridegroom.
+ **1618-1620** Vocation of virginity for the sake of the kingdom.

✝ **1471-1479** The "temporal punishments of sin," the communion of saints and indulgences for the faithful departed.

THIRTY-THIRD SUNDAY OF ORDINARY TIME (330a)

READING:

Proverbs 31:10-13, 19, 20, 30-31 The worthy wife is a treasure. Working with loving hands, extending herself to the needy and fearing the Lord.

Psalm 128 Blessed are those who fear the Lord.

1 Thessalonians 5:1-6 The day of the Lord comes like a thief at night. As children of the light, do not sleep but stay alert and sober.

Matthew 25:14-30 (or 14-15, 19-21) The servants and the talents. "Well done. Since you have been faithful in small matters, come share your master's joy."

CATECHISM:

+ **1023-1029** Looking to be with Christ in heaven.
+ **673-677** The Church's final trial in expectation of Christ's glory: imminent but delayed.
+ **678-679, 1038-1041** Christ the judge and the final judgment.
+ **2846-2849** "Lead us not into temptation" and the grace of final perseverance.
+ **1936-1937** Varied human "talents" are to be shared.
+ **2683-2684** The saints as witnesses in prayer. "Entering their master's joy," they have been "put in charge of many things."

CHRIST THE KING

READING:

Ezekiel 34:11-12, 15-17 I myself will tend my sheep. I will rescue them and give them rest, judging between rams and goats.

Psalm 23 The Lord is my shepherd; there is nothing I shall want.

1 Corinthians 15:20-26, 28 Christ, the New Adam, is raised as the first fruits of the dead. After subduing every principality and power – including death – he will submit himself to the Father so that God can be all in all.

Matthew 25:31-46 The Son of Man, sitting on his royal throne, will separate all the nations into two groups for their final destiny. "For I was hungry…"

CATECHISM:

+ **632-635** Christ's descent into hell.
+ **655** Christ's Resurrection: the source for ours.
+ **668-672, 1008** The ascended Christ already reigns and is at work renewing the world by subjecting all things to himself – even death.
+ **294, 1050** Creation's destiny: Christ presents to the Father a transfigured world where God may be "all in all."
+ **1326, 1397, 1403-1405** In the Eucharistic celebration, we are committed to caring for the presence of Christ in the poor, and we anticipate our final and perfect communion.

+ **544, 1033, 1932, 2447** Jesus is met in the poor and lowly. Our care for them is a condition for entering his kingdom. The works of mercy.

+ **678-679, 1038-1039** Judged by our choices before Christ the judge.

+ **257, 260, 1027-1029, 1034-1035, 1720-1721** Our fate in heaven's joy or "eternal fire."

TRANSFIGURATION OF THE LORD (AUGUST 6)

READING:

Daniel 7:9-10, 13-14 Ancient one. Myriads attended. Son of Man given rule.

Psalm 97 The Lord is king, the most high over all the earth.

2 Peter 1:16-19 Not myths: we ourselves heard, saw his splendor.

Matthew 17:1-9 Transfigured on mountain. Good! "My Son!"

CATECHISM:

+ **554-556** Transfiguration: a foretaste of the kingdom.
+ **422-424, 606-608** The whole life of the Beloved Son among us is an offering to the Father.
+ **660-664** The glory and dominion of the Risen One at the Father's right hand.
+ **2794-2796** The majesty of the Father who is "in heaven."
+ **2583** Moses and Elijah: finding God in varied ways, now they see the unveiled face of Christ.

ASSUMPTION OF THE BLESSED VIRGIN

READING:

Revelation 11:19, 12:1-6, 10 Great sign: woman clothed with the sun. Her newborn child is saved from the devouring dragon.

Psalm 45 The queen stands at your right hand, arrayed in gold.

1 Corinthians 15:20-26 In Adam all die. In Christ all will come to life as he conquers every enemy, even death itself.

Luke 1:39-56 Visit to Elizabeth. "Blessed is she who believed." Magnificat.

CATECHISM:

+ **1138** Celebrants of the heavenly liturgy.
+ **410-412, 495, 655, 1008** Adam's death and Mary, the New Eve. Christ's Resurrection and the destiny of his Church.
+ **668, 671-672** Christ reigns until all things are subjected to him. The distress of the Church as it waits.
+ **717, 721-726** The Holy Spirit works in Mary, the New Eve.
+ **273, 2617-2619** The prayer of the Virgin Mary.
+ **964-970** Mary: united with Christ — also in her assumption — is our Mother in the order of grace.

SOLEMNITY OF ALL SAINTS

READING:

Revelation 7:2-4, 9-14 A crowd that no one could number — they washed their robes in blood of Lamb.

Psalm 24 Lord, this is the people that longs to see your face.

1 John 3:1-3 The Father's love. We are God's children now. Then we will be like him.

Matthew 5:1-12 On the mountain, Jesus teaches the beatitudes.

CATECHISM:

+ **1138, 2642** The heavenly liturgy. Its celebrants, its prayer of praise.
+ **1296** The "seal" of God's servants (confirmation).
+ **163-164** Faith: tasting in advance the beatific vision, even amid trials.
+ **1023-1024** Heaven: seeing God face to face. Communion of life and love with the Most Holy Trinity.
+ **1161** Mary and the saints: participants in world's salvation and in communion with us (Holy Images).
+ **1716-1724** Our vocation to beatitude.
+ **520** Christ, our model of holiness.
+ **828-829, 946-948, 954-957, 1173** The Church is holy. The communion of saints. Memorials of the saints.
+ **1474-1477** Sharing the treasury of the communion of saints (relating to indulgences).
+ **2683-2684** The saints as examples of prayer.

+ *Cycle B*

FIRST SUNDAY OF ADVENT (1*Ab*)

READING:

Isaiah 63:16-17, 19, 64:2-7 Return, O Lord. Do not let us wander. Our good deeds are like polluted rags. Rend the heavens and come down! We are the clay, you the potter.

Psalm 80 Lord, make us turn to you. Let us see your face, and we shall be saved.

1 Corinthians 1:3-9 Grace from God! You have been enriched in every way as you wait for the Lord.

Mark 13:33-37 Be alert. Watch so that the master will not find you sleeping.

CATECHISM:

+ **300-301** God, transcending creation, remains present to it and sustains it.
+ **385-387** The burden of sin hangs upon us.
+ **672, 678-679** Keep watch. The judgment on the day of the Lord.
+ **1731-1738** Human freedom and responsibility. Choosing between good and evil. The "slavery of sin."
+ **2612, 2632, 2816-2827** God's people pray: "Thy kingdom come, thy will be done on earth as in heaven!"

IMMACULATE CONCEPTION

READING:

Genesis 3:9-15, 20 After eating from the tree, Adam hid in fear. The woman reveals, "The serpent tricked me into it, so I ate it." God declared enmity between her offspring and the serpent's.

Psalm 98 Sing to the Lord a new song, for he has done marvelous deeds.

Ephesians 1:3-6, 11-12 God chose us before the foundation of the world to be holy and blameless.

Luke 1:26-38 The angel Gabriel announces to Mary: "Hail, full of grace!"

CATECHISM:

+ **374-379** Adam and Eve in Paradise.
+ **385-390** The Fall. Where sin abounded, grace abounded all the more. Reality of sin and original sin.
+ **397-400** Original sin: Loss of holiness and harmony. Distorted image of God.
+ **490-494** The Immaculate Conception.

SECOND SUNDAY OF ADVENT (2*Ab*)

READING:

Isaiah 40:1-5, 9-11 Comfort my people. Speak tenderly to her. "Prepare a way for the Lord."

Psalm 85 Lord, let us see your kindness and grant us your salvation.

2 Peter 3:8-14 The day of the Lord will come with judgment. Await and hasten that day by remaining holy and undefiled.

Mark 1:1-8 John appeared, proclaiming a baptism of repentance in expectation of the coming of him who will baptize in the Holy Spirit.

CATECHISM:

✝ **976-980,1262-1266** One baptism for forgiveness of sins. Regeneration and a new life.
✝ **1739-1742** Human freedom and economy of salvation. Freedom and sin. Threats to freedom. Liberation and salvation. Freedom and grace.
✝ **2525-2527** Purification of the social climate (Ninth Commandment).

THIRD SUNDAY OF ADVENT (3*Ab*)

READING:

Isaiah 61: 1-2, 10-11 Rejoice in the Lord heartily.

(Psalm) Luke 1:46 ff. My soul rejoices in my God.

1 Thessalonians 5:16-24 May you be preserved blameless for the coming of the Lord.

John 1:6-8, 19-28 John witnesses to the one to come who will proclaim freedom and deliverance.

CATECHISM:

✝ **2012-2016** Christian holiness (call to intimate union with God). Ascetical dimension. Grace of final perseverance.

✝ **759-769** The Church: Born in Father's heart, foreshadowed from the beginning, prepared for in Old Covenant, inaugurated by Christ.

✝ **1285-1289, 1303** Baptismal grace is completed in the anointing of the Holy Spirit in confirmation. The call to proclaim the Good News.

FOURTH SUNDAY OF ADVENT (4*Ab*)

READING:

2 Samuel 7:1-5, 8-11, 16 I took you from the pasture to make you leader, O Israel. Your house will endure, and your heir will sit upon your throne.

Psalm 89 Forever I will sing the goodness of the Lord.

Romans 16:25-27 The mystery kept secret is now manifest to all nations. To the only wise God, through Jesus Christ, be glory for ever.

Luke 1:26-38 Gabriel speaks to Mary: You will bear a son and name him Jesus. He will rule from the throne of David.

CATECHISM:

+ **464-469** Jesus: True God and True Man (some early heresies).
+ **148-149, 273-274, 494, 2617-2619** "With God nothing is impossible": the example of Mary's faith and prayer.
+ **721-726** Spirit's role to fulfill the Father's plan in Mary.

THE NATIVITY OF THE LORD (CHRISTMAS)

READING:

Given the vast scope and great riches of the Scriptures proclaimed in the Nativity of the Lord, there is no attempt here to refer to particular passages. Instead, some overarching theological themes are offered.

CATECHISM:

+ **65-67** Finality of the revelation of the Word-made-flesh.
+ **456-469** Why did the Word become flesh? Jesus is not "part God and part man."
+ **525-526** The Christmas mystery.

THE HOLY FAMILY OF JESUS, MARY, AND JOSEPH

READING:

Sirach 3:2-6, 12-14 Father and mother are to be honored.

Psalm 128 Blessed are those who fear the Lord and walk in his ways.

Colossians 3:12-21 As God's chosen ones, live in harmony and thankfulness. **Or Genesis 15:1-6, 21:1-3** The Lord promises Abram that his descendants will outnumber the stars.

Psalm 105 The Lord remembers his covenant forever.

Hebrews 11:8, 11-12, 17-19 Abraham and Sarah journeyed in faith.

Luke 2:22-40 (or 2:22, 39-40) Jesus is presented in the temple. He grew and became strong, filled with wisdom.

CATECHISM:

+ **2685** Family: first place of prayer.
+ **529** The presentation in the temple.
+ **1156-1158** Tradition of singing when we pray.
+ **2207-2213** Family: original cell of social life. To be protected. Illuminates other relationships and life in community.
+ **1674-1676** Religious custom. "Popular piety."

SOLEMNITY OF THE BLESSED VIRGIN MARY, MOTHER OF GOD

READING:

Numbers 6:22-27 The Lord's name was to be invoked upon the people in blessing: "The Lord bless you and keep you."

Psalm 67 May God bless us in his mercy.

Galatians 4:4-7 In the fullness of time, God sent his Son, born of a woman.

Luke 2:16-21 The shepherds went to Bethlehem and found Mary and Joseph and the infant lying in the manger. Mary reflected on all these things in her heart.

CATECHISM:

✝ **484-489** Jesus: "Conceived by the power of the Holy Spirit; born of the Virgin Mary."

✝ **495** Mary's divine motherhood.

✝ **502-507** Mary's virginal motherhood in God's plan. God's absolute initiative. A new birth for New Adam. Sign of Mary's faith unmixed with doubt. Image of Church.

EPIPHANY

READING:

Isaiah 60:1-6 Rise up in splendor. The glory of the Lord shines upon you.

Psalm 72 Lord, every nation on earth will adore you.

Ephesians 3:2-3, 5-6 The mystery made known: The Gentiles are coheirs of the promise.

Matthew 2:1-12 Magi from the East arrived. "We saw his star." Finding the child, they offered their gifts.

CATECHISM:

+ **830-845** Who belongs to the Church? The Church and non-Christians.
+ **528** The mystery of Epiphany.
+ **771-776** The Church: visible and spiritual. Sacrament of universal salvation.
+ **846-848** "Outside the Church there is no salvation."
+ **1163-1165, 1168-1173** Liturgical year and seasons. Noting the tradition of announcing the year's movable feasts at Epiphany.

BAPTISM OF THE LORD

READING:

Isaiah 42:1-4, 6-7 Here is my servant, called for the victory of justice.

Psalm 29 The Lord will bless his people with peace.

Acts 10:34-38 God shows no partiality. He proclaimed peace through Jesus Christ, beginning after John's baptism, when Jesus was anointed with the Holy Spirit.

Mark:1 7-11 "You are my beloved Son; with you I am well pleased."

CATECHISM:

+ **535-537** The mystery of the baptism of Jesus.
+ **1226-1229** Baptism in the Church. Essential elements in the initiation journey: Word, acceptance, conversion, faith, baptism, outpouring of Holy Spirit, admission to Eucharist.
+ **2560** Prayer as human thirst encountering God's thirst for us.

FIRST SUNDAY OF LENT (1Lb)

READING:

Genesis 9:8-15 God's covenant with Noah when Noah was delivered from the flood.

Psalm 25 Your ways, O Lord, are love and truth to those who keep your covenant.

1 Peter 3:18-22 The waters of baptism bring salvation and forgiveness through the death of Christ.

Mark 1:12-15 Following a fast of forty days and being put to test, the public ministry of Jesus begins.

CATECHISM:

+ **1440-1449** The Sacrament of Penance: God's deed in and through the Church.
+ **538-540** Temptations of Jesus.
+ **845-848** Church as ark. No salvation apart from that that is manifest in the Church.
+ **1078-1082** The Father: source of the covenant of blessing.
+ **1219-1220** Noah's ark: baptismal image.
+ **1226-1228** Baptism in the Church.

SECOND SUNDAY OF LENT (2Lb)

READING:

Genesis 22:1-2, 9, 10-13, 15-18 Ready even to sacrifice Isaac, Abraham is our father in faith.

Psalm 116 I will walk before the Lord, in the land of the living.

Romans 8:31-34 It is Jesus who died and was raised for us all.

Mark 9:2-10 In his transfiguration, Jesus is revealed as God's Son.

CATECHISM:

+ **101-104** Christ, unique Word of Scripture.
+ **131-133** Scripture in life of Church.
+ **1810-1821** Virtue and grace. Virtues of faith and hope. Abraham's hope.
+ **2570-2572** Abraham's faith does not weaken.

THIRD SUNDAY OF LENT (3Lb)

READING:

Exodus 20:1-17 or 20:1-3, 7-8, 12-17 "In those days, God delivered all these commandments."

Psalm 19 Lord, you have the words of everlasting life.

1 Corinthians 1:22-25 "Signs," "wisdom," and the cross.

John 2:13-25 Jesus is the sign of the power and wisdom of God the Father.

CATECHISM:

+ **272** Mystery of God's apparent powerlessness.
+ **583-586** Jesus and the temple.
+ **2056-2063** The Decalogue.
+ **1961-1964** The Old Law.
+ **2112-2114** Confronting "idolatry."
+ **2580** Jerusalem temple.
+ **1179-1181, 1186** The purpose of church buildings.

FOURTH SUNDAY OF LENT (4Lb)

READING:

2 Chronicles 36:14-16, 19-23 Judah's infidelity led to the exile from which God, in mercy, led them home.

Psalm 137 Let my tongue be silenced if I ever forget you.

Ephesians 2:4-10 Despite transgressions, God, rich in mercy, offers saving grace.

John 3:14-21 Jesus to Nicodemus: "The Son of Man must be lifted up; God so loved the world..."

CATECHISM:

✝ **218-221, 604-605** God is love. God takes the initiative in universal love – in Christ, whose death is for all without exception.

✝ **309-314** Providence and scandal of evil.

✝ **456-458** God gives his Son for us.

✝ **709-710** God's Spirit at work even in the breakup and exile of Israel.

✝ **845-848, 1257-1261** Necessity of baptism.

✝ **1996-1997** Grace: God's help and participation in God's life.

✝ **2002** Longing for truth and goodness. Our free response to God's grace-filled initiative.

FIFTH SUNDAY OF LENT (5Lb)

READING:

Jeremiah 31:31-34 The new covenant, "I will be their God, and they shall be my people."

Psalm 51 Create a clean heart in me, O God.

Hebrews 5:7-9 Through suffering, Christ learned obedience and became the source of eternal salvation.

John 12:20-33 The grain of wheat must die to produce much fruit.

CATECHISM:

+ **599-605** Christ's death and God's saving plan.
+ **434** Resurrection glorifies the name of the Savior God.
+ **606-609, 616-617** Christ offered himself to Father, even on the cross.
+ **662** The "lifting up" of Christ.

PASSION SUNDAY

PROCESSION:

Mark 11:1-10 or John 12:12-16 Entrance to Jerusalem.

READING:

Isaiah 50:4-7 I gave my back to those who beat me. The Lord is my help. I have set my face like flint, knowing that I shall not be put to shame.

Psalm 22 My God, my God, why have you abandoned me?

Philippians 2:6-11 Christ humbled himself, obedient even to death on a cross. God greatly exalted him.

Mark 14:1-15:47 or 15:1-39 The Passion of our Lord Jesus Christ.

CATECHISM:

+ **449** Divine title "Lord."
+ **571-572** "He was crucified under Pontius Pilate": the Paschal mystery is the heart of the Good News.
+ **595-598** The trial of Jesus. Jews not collectively responsible for death of Jesus, but rather all sinners.
+ **613-618** Jesus' obedience unto death, sacrifice consummated on cross.
+ **2099-2100** Offering sacrifice to God.
+ **557-560** Jesus' entry into Jerusalem.

HOLY THURSDAY EVENING MASS OF THE LORD'S SUPPER

READING:

Exodus 12:1-8, 11-14 The Israelites prepared and shared the sacrificial lamb like those who are in flight. "It is the Passover of the Lord."

Psalm 116 Our blessing-cup is a communion with the Blood of Christ.

1 Corinthians 11:23-26 As often as you eat this bread and drink the cup, you proclaim the death of the Lord until he comes.

John 13:1-15 The hour has come. Jesus loved them to the end. "I have given you a model. . . . As I have done for you, you should also do."

CATECHISM:

> **Glory in the cross of Christ**
> + **606-607** Christ freely embraces the will of his Father.
> + **608-609** The Lamb of God loves his own to the end.
> + **610-611** At supper with his friends, Christ anticipates the free offering of his life.
> + **612** The sacrificial cup of Gethsemane.
> + **613-614** The sacrificial death of the Lamb of God.
> + **615-618** Christ's obedience even to death, loving his own to the end. Our share in his sacrifice.
> + **440, 520, 786** The "Christ," our model. His royalty revealed in service.

✝ **2746-2750** Christ's prayer when "the hour" had come.

The Eucharist instituted

✝ **1322-1327** The perpetuation of the sacrifice of the cross. Completes our initiation into Christ.

✝ **1334, 1337-1344** The Holy Eucharist. Rooted in the Passover event and Christ's own Passover. Done in memory of him "until he comes."

✝ **1356-1368** The Church carries out the Lord's command, offering the sacrifice of praise to the Father and the memorial of Christ's Passover.

✝ **1380-1381** The event of his Passion. Facing his departure in bodily form, Christ gives the sacrament of his true presence.

✝ **1382-1384, 1403** Eating and drinking the Paschal banquet. Awaiting its fulfillment in God's kingdom.

The Priesthood of Christ continues in his Church

✝ **1544-1545** Christ, true and only priest of the New Covenant, offers his redemptive sacrifice on the cross.

✝ **1546-1548** Christ's priesthood continues in the community of believers and, uniquely, in the ministerial priesthood.

✝ **1066-1068** The work of salvation, principally in the Paschal mystery, is manifest in the liturgy.

✝ **1085, 1088-1089** Christ is active in the liturgy, associating the Church with himself in making present his Paschal mystery.

GOOD FRIDAY OF THE
LORD'S PASSION

READING:

Isaiah 52:13-53:12 God's servant. Wounded for our sins, carrying the guilt of all.

Psalm 31 Father, into your hands I commend my spirit.

Hebrews 4:14-16, 5:7-9 Jesus, the great high priest, tested in every way, yet without sin. He learned obedience from what he suffered and became the source of eternal salvation.

John 18:1-19:42 The Passion of our Lord Jesus Christ.

CATECHISM:

+ **711-716, 1505** Christ: God's servant, taking the form of a slave, yet anointed in the Spirit to bring freedom, healing, and peace to the poor.
+ **595-598** The trial of Jesus. Responsibility for his death.
+ **599-600** Christ's violent death. Not outside the plan of God.
+ **601-603** Christ, the sinless one, suffers for our sins.
+ **604-605** God takes the initiative in redeeming love.
+ **1992, 2305** Justification by the cross of Christ. Christ makes peace on the cross.
+ **766** The Church is born of Christ's total self-giving, coming forth from his side as he died on the cross.

EASTER VIGIL

READING:

Given the vast scope and great riches of the Scriptures proclaimed in the Great Vigil, there is no attempt here to refer to particular passages. Instead, some overarching theological themes of this night are offered.

CATECHISM:

+ **142, 260, 460** God's fundamental purpose: The entrance of his creatures into the perfect communion of the Holy Trinity.

+ **290-301** Creation: Work of the Trinity, for God's glory, upheld by God.

+ **355-361** Humanity: image of God. Restored in the New Adam.

+ **396-404, 412** Sin brings death into human history. "O happy fault."

+ **603-605, 2572** God manifests benevolent, all-embracing love as he gives his beloved Son (prefigured in the sacrifice of Isaac).

+ **624-628** Christ in the tomb. Our baptismal union with him there.

+ **272, 638, 647, 654** Resurrection: God's power in apparent powerlessness. The crowning truth of our faith. The "truly blessed night." Its meaning for us.

+ **1214-1222, 1225** Baptism: plunging into Christ's death, regeneration, and enlightenment. Rooted in history of salvation and Christ's Passover.

+ **1262-1674** Baptism for the forgiveness of sins. A new creation. Incorporation into Christ. Union with other believers. Consecration for religious worship.

+ **1362-1364** Paschal "remembrance." Christ's Passover made present in the Eucharist.

+ **1612, 1617** Initiation into a nuptial union between God and his people.

+ **2560-2565** Prayer: Christ meets us at the well where we go in our thirst. Our covenant "from the heart." Our communion.

+ **62-64, 759-766** The formation of God's people in covenant. Expectation of renewal. Gathering the scattered children. The mystery of the Church revealed from creation to the cross.

EASTER SUNDAY

READING:

Acts 10:34, 37-43 Peter preaches. In the Holy Sprit, Jesus brought goodness and healing. They put him to death, but God raised him. We who ate and drank with him after he rose from the dead are his witnesses.

Psalm 118 This is the day the Lord has made; let us rejoice and be glad.

Colossians 3:1-4 Raised with Christ, seek what is above, where Christ is. **Or 1 Corinthians 5:6-8** Clear out the old yeast that you may become fresh dough. Christ, our Paschal lamb, has been sacrificed.

John 20:1-9 Mary went to the tomb and found it empty. Peter and John then came and saw the burial cloths, for Christ had to rise from the dead. **Or (at afternoon or evening Masses) Luke 24:13-35** The road to Emmaus. They recognized him in the breaking of bread.

CATECHISM:

+ **651-655** Saving power of Christ's Resurrection.
+ **648-650** Trinitarian work of the Resurrection.
+ **1262-1269** Effects of baptism. Forgiveness of sins. "New creature." Incorporation into Church.

When Luke's Emmaus Gospel is read:
+ **601** Christ's saving death was in accord with the Scriptures.
+ **1329, 1347** The Risen One reveals himself in the Eucharist.

SECOND SUNDAY OF EASTER (2Eb)

READING:

Acts 4:32-35 The community was of one mind and heart, with no needy person among them because they shared all.

Psalm 118 Give thanks to the Lord for he is good. His love is everlasting.

1 John 5:1-6 Those who believe in Christ are begotten of God, keep his commandments, and conquer the world.

John 20:19-31 The risen Lord meets with the disciples, shares the Holy Spirit. Thomas is absent and will not believe until he sees.

CATECHISM:

✝ **210-211, 478** God's Son has been lifted up and reveals that God's mercy endures forever. The heart of Christ: loving us to the end.

✝ **1461-1462, 1468-1470** Sacramental reconciliation: restoring intimate friendship with God, a "spiritual resurrection." Christ entrusts the forgiveness of sins to his ministers.

✝ **644-646** The disciples' doubts. The condition of Christ's resurrected humanity.

✝ **728-730** In the hour of his glorification, Christ breathes forth the Holy Spirit to share his mission with his Church.

✝ **820-822** Maintaining the unity of the Church.

✝ **949-953, 2043** Church: a communion in spiritual and temporal goods. Precept to provide for needs of the Church.

+ **1097-1098** In the liturgy, the faithful — drawn in the Spirit beyond differences of race and culture — encounter Christ.

+ **1846-1848** God's mercy to sinners.

THIRD SUNDAY OF EASTER (3*Eb*)

READING:

Acts 3:13-15, 17-19 You denied the Righteous One and in ignorance put to death the author of life. So repent, that your sins may be wiped away.

Psalm 4 Lord, let your face shine on us.

1 John 2:1-5 If any should sin, we have Jesus, an Advocate with the Father and expiation for the whole world's sins.

Luke 24:35-48 The risen Jesus appears again: "Peace!" To allay their fears, he lets the disciples touch him, and he eats with them. It was written that the Christ would suffer and be raised from the dead. You are witnesses of this.

CATECHISM:

> + **597-598** Sinners bear responsibility for Christ's death.
> + **519, 601** Christ, our advocate who always intercedes for us, died for our sins.
> + **654** Resurrection reinstates us in God's grace so that we might walk in newness of life.
> + **1362-1367** Eucharist as memorial of Christ's Passover.
> + **1168-1171** Easter as the heart of the Church year: All of life stands in the light of the Paschal mystery.

FOURTH SUNDAY OF EASTER (4Eb)

READING:

Acts 4:8-12 The apostles healed in the name of Jesus Christ. There is no salvation through anyone else.

Psalm 118 The stone rejected by the builders has become the cornerstone.

1 John 3:1-2 What love from the Father! We are God's children. We shall see God as he is.

John 10:11-18 I am the Good Shepherd, who lays down his life for his sheep. I know mine, and they know me. There will be one flock and one shepherd.

CATECHISM:

+ **946-953** Church as communion of saints.
+ **604-606, 609** Christ freely laid down his life for all of us.
+ **817-819** Wounds to the unity of the Church.
+ **1396** Eucharist and the Church's unity.
+ **432, 1507** The name "Jesus" means savior.
+ **845-848** Salvation through Christ alone and through the one Church, his body.
+ **163, 460** Faith: beginning of eternal life. Our divine adoption.
+ **1213-1216, 1257-1261, 1265-1266** Baptism. Freedom from sin. Rebirth as God's children. The necessity of enlightenment.
+ **1996-1999** Grace: participation in life of God. "Sanctifying" and "divinizing."

FIFTH SUNDAY OF EASTER (5*Eb*)

READING:

Acts 9:26-31 The disciples were afraid of Saul until Barnabas reported about how he saw the Lord. Saul speaks boldly about Christ.

Psalm 22 I will praise you, Lord, in the assembly of your people.

1 John 3:18-24 Believe in Jesus and love not in word only but in deed. Keep this commandment and remain in him.

John 15:1-8 Branches on the true vine: Bear much fruit.

CATECHISM:

+ **1267-1274** Baptism configures us to Christ, brings a share in his priesthood and communion with other Christians.
+ **1091-1092, 1108, 1988** Holy Spirit is "life of the vine." Grafts us onto Christ so that we may live from the life of the risen Christ.
+ **755, 787-789** Church as communion with Christ, the vine.
+ **737, 2074** Bearing "fruit" in Christ.
+ **1114-1119** The body of Christ: source of the saving power of the sacraments. The Church forms one mystical person with Christ.
+ **2767-2772, 2777-2778** In the liturgical assembly we dare to pray, "Our Father."

SIXTH SUNDAY OF EASTER (6Eb)

READING:

Acts 10:25-26, 34-35, 44-48 Peter addressed Cornelius, and the Holy Spirit came upon all — so they were baptized in the name of Jesus Christ.

Psalm 98 The Lord has revealed to the nations his saving power.

1 John 4:7-10 Let us love one another for God is love.

John 15:9-17 Remain in my love. My commandment: love one another as I have loved you, laying down my life. I chose you to go and bear fruit.

CATECHISM:

+ **25, 864, 1889** Motivated by the love that never ends to selfless charity.
+ **142-143, 218-221** God is love. God speaks to all as friends and invites them to share his life in faith.
+ **434-435** Prayer in the name of the risen Christ.
+ **733-736, 2615, 2745** God's love poured out in the Holy Spirit, nurtures "much fruit."
+ **609, 1822-1825, 1972** Christ's perfect love and his new commandment.
+ **761, 1226** Baptism is given to those prepared by faith and repentance.
+ **1306-1311** Preparing for confirmation: The baptized "live on" in the love of Christ.

SOLEMNITY OF THE ASCENSION OF THE LORD

READING:

Acts 1:1-11 After appearing to them through forty days, the risen Christ was lifted up. They were to await the baptism with the Holy Spirit.

Psalm 47 God mounts his throne to shouts of joy: a blare of trumpets for the Lord.

Ephesians 1:17-23 May God's power work in you — the power that raised Christ from the dead, seated him at God's right hand, and placed all things under his feet. **Or Ephesians 4:1-13 (or 4:1-7, 11-13)** Live according to your calling. Christ ascended that he might fill all things. He gives gifts of service to build up the body to the full stature of Christ.

Mark 16:15-20 "Proclaim the Gospel to every creature." Great signs will accompany believers. Then Jesus was taken up to heaven, and they went forth everywhere.

CATECHISM:

+ **673-674** Since the Ascension: expectation of Christ's glorious coming as we grow to his full stature.
+ **648** The Father's power "raised up" Christ and introduced his humanity into the Trinity.
+ **668-672, 1673, 2045** Christ reigns and fills the Church, his body. Yet his rule is not fulfilled in power until all things are subjected to him.
+ **1226-1227** Mission to baptize.

+ **161, 1256-1261** Necessity of faith in Christ and baptism.

+ **434** Resurrection of Christ glorifies the name of the Savior God.

+ **2632** Prayer of petition: first of all for the kingdom to come.

+ **814** Church's unity in multiplicity.

+ **632-635** Christ's "descent" to the dead.

SEVENTH SUNDAY OF EASTER (7*Eb*)

READING:

Acts 1:15-17, 20-26 The apostles identify Matthias to take the place of Judas, to join those who accompanied Jesus and witnessed his Resurrection.

Psalm 103 The Lord has set his throne in heaven.

1 John 4:11-16 Whoever remains in love remains in God and God in him.

John 17:11-19 "Father, keep them in your name that they may be one. Consecrate them in truth."

CATECHISM:

+ **642, 858-861** Apostolic witness to the Resurrection: fundamental to Church.
+ **221, 604, 733, 1828** God is love. Our response.
+ **772-773** Church: human communion with God.
+ **611, 2747-2748, 2812** Christ's "priestly prayer." Consecrated to the Father, unity.
+ **2815, 2846, 2849-2850** The Lord's Prayer: protection in God's name from the evil one.
+ **215-217, 2466** God is truth. Living in truth.
+ **888-892** Church abides in truth through the ministry of the Magisterium.

PENTECOST

VIGIL (CATECHISM):

2655-2658 Prayer: internalizes the liturgy and relies on faith, hope, and love.

READING:

Acts 2:1-11 They were all filled with the Holy Spirit and began to speak. All who heard them heard in their native language.

Psalm 104 Lord, send out your Spirit, and renew the face of the earth.

1 Corinthians 12:3-7, 12-13 Different gifts, but the same Spirit. In one Spirit we were all baptized into one body, able to say "Jesus is Lord." **Or Galatians 5:16-25** Live by the Spirit — avoiding the bitter works of the flesh and cultivating the fruits of the Spirit.

John 20:19-23 The risen Jesus meets his disciples: "Peace be with you. As the Father has sent me, I send you. Receive the Holy Spirit. Whose sins you forgive are forgiven them." **Or John 15:26-27, 16:12-15** The Advocate, the Spirit of truth will guide you to all truth — declaring to you what he takes from me.

CATECHISM:

+ **687-690, 730** Holy Spirit: presence. Joint mission with Christ.
+ **733-741, 1695** The Spirit: God's gift and source of Church's mission. Sign of justification.

+ **2515-2516, 2541-2543, 2819, 2848** The struggle of the flesh and the spirit.
+ **797-801** Church as "Temple of the Spirit": alive, united, and gifted in the Spirit.
+ **91-92, 243-244, 729, 2615** Guided by the Spirit to all truth.
+ **1442** Church: sign and instrument of forgiveness.

SOLEMNITY OF THE MOST HOLY TRINITY

READING:

Deuteronomy 4:32-34, 39-40 Moses tells the people: Consider God's great deeds for you. The Lord is God, there is no other. So keep his statutes and live.

Psalm 33 Blessed the people the Lord has chosen to be his own.

Romans 8:14-17 Those led by Spirit are sons of God. Heirs with Christ, we cry out "Abba, Father."

Matthew 28:16-20 The great commission: make disciples of the nations, baptizing them in the name of the Father, the Son, and the Holy Spirit.

CATECHISM:

+ **238-245** Revelation of the mystery of the Trinity.
+ **257-260** How God acts — the Trinity at work.
+ **850** Church's mission: bring people to share in communion of Holy Trinity.
+ **2779-2783** "Our Father!"
+ **189-190** Trinitarian nature of the baptismal profession of faith.

SOLEMNITY OF THE MOST HOLY BODY AND BLOOD OF CHRIST

READING:

Exodus 24:3-8 To seal the covenant, Moses poured out the sacrificial blood: half on the altar, half on the people.

Psalm 116 I will take the cup of salvation and call on the name of the Lord.

Hebrews 9:11-15 Christ the priest entered the perfect tabernacle with his own blood as sacrifice, cleansing us from dead works. He is mediator of a New Covenant.

Mark 14:12-16, 22-26 Jesus shares the Passover meal in the upper room. "Take, this is my body; this is my blood of the covenant."

CATECHISM:

+ **1104-1109** The liturgy. Saving deeds made present now through Holy Spirit.
+ **610-614, 1362-1365, 1390, 1403** Christ's paschal sacrifice: New Covenant sealed in his blood.
+ **662** Christ: true priest of the eternal covenant.
+ **1084-1090** Christ's presence and paschal mystery in the Church's liturgy.
+ **1140-1144, 1368** The liturgy: celebrated by those who, in various ways, participate in the one priesthood of Christ.
+ **1566** In the Eucharistic sacrifice, the ordained priest finds the greatest exercise of and inspiration for his office.

SECOND SUNDAY OF ORDINARY TIME (20b)

READING:

1 Samuel 3:3-10, 19 The Lord calls young Samuel in the night: "Speak, Lord, your servant is listening."

Psalm 40 Here am I, Lord. I come to do your will.

1 Corinthians 6:13-15, 17-20 The body is for the Lord. You are members of Christ.

John 1:35-42 "Look, the Lamb of God." "Where do you stay?" "Come and see."

CATECHISM:

+ **523, 606-608** The "Lamb who takes away the sin of the world." Jesus comes to do the Father's will.

+ **1546-1547** Christ incorporates the baptized into his mission of priest, prophet, king. He further and uniquely shares himself through the ministerial priesthood.

+ **2578** Samuel learns prayerful listening for God's voice.

+ **364, 1004, 2331-2359** The body is to be honored. It participates in Christ's dignity. The vocation of chastity (Sixth Commandment).

+ **1265, 1269, 1694-1695** The baptized are incorporated into Christ, belong now to him and are called to be saints and temples of the Holy Spirit.

+ **1709** Faith transforms us so that we can follow Christ.

THIRD SUNDAY OF
ORDINARY TIME (30b)

READING:

Jonah 3:1-5, 10 The Ninevites listened to the preaching of Jonah and repented of their evil ways.

Psalm 25 Teach me your ways, O Lord. The world in its present form is passing away.

1 Corinthians 7:29-31 The world in its present form is passing away.

Mark 1:14-20 Repent! Believe in the Gospel.

CATECHISM:

✝ **1619** Virginity as sign of expectation of Christ's coming.
✝ **1427** Jesus calls to conversion.
✝ **541-543** The "time of fulfillment": gathering people into God's family. Open to everyone, including sinners.
✝ **1577-1580** Ministerial priesthood: conferred on men. Not a right but a call. Latin Rite/Eastern Rite disciplines of celibacy.
✝ **874-876** Christ as source of ministry in Church.

FOURTH SUNDAY OF
ORDINARY TIME (4Ob)

READING:

Deuteronomy 18:15-20 Moses challenges the Israelites to listen to God's voice.

Psalm 95 If today you hear his voice, harden not your hearts.

1 Corinthians 7:32-35 Be concerned about the things of the Lord that you may be holy.

Mark 1:21-28 Jesus taught them as one having authority.

CATECHISM:

+ **1554-1561** Bishops, like the apostles, receive the Holy Spirit for their work and care for a portion of God's people. Priests, too, share the universal mission of Christ given to the apostles.
+ **914-933, 1579, 2349** The consecrated life. Celibacy for the sake of the kingdom. Chastity suited to state in life.
+ **436, 547-550** The "Christ": prophet, priest, and king. The significance of his liberating signs.
+ **1672-1673** Consecrations for God's service. Exorcism: the invocation of God's protection.

FIFTH SUNDAY OF ORDINARY TIME (50b)

READING:

Job 7:1-4, 6-7 Job, filled with restlessness, cries out.

Psalm 147:1-2, 3-4, 5-6 Praise the Lord, who heals the brokenhearted.

1 Corinthians 9:16-19, 22-23 Preach the Good News of the Gospel.

Mark 1:29-39 Jesus is the hope of those who put their trust in him.

CATECHISM:

> ✝ **547-550** Healing: a messianic sign.
> ✝ **1499-1505** Human sickness and Christ the Physician.
> ✝ **1562-1571** Priests: configured to Christ, the head of the body. Fulfill apostolic mission as co-workers with bishops. Forming a sacramental order or "college." Deacons: configured to Christ, the servant of all.
> ✝ **2276-2283** Defending life when it is diminished or troubled: euthanasia, suicide (Fifth Commandment).

SIXTH SUNDAY OF ORDINARY TIME (6*Ob*)

READING:

Leviticus 13:1-2, 44-46 The leper is forced to dwell apart from the community.

Psalm 32 I turn to you, Lord, in time of trouble, and you fill me with the joy of salvation.

1 Corinthians 10:31-11:1 Be imitators of Christ.

Mark 1:40-45 Turning to Jesus in need, the leper is cured and filled with joy.

CATECHISM:

+ **1581-1584** Ordained minister receives an irrevocable configuring to Christ, who acts through him in a special way.
+ **1505-1510** Healing: sign of the kingdom.
+ **1520-1523** Effects of sacramental anointing.
+ **2616** Jesus hears prayers.
+ **2288-2291** Proper concern for health.

SEVENTH SUNDAY OF ORDINARY TIME (7Ob)

READING:

Isaiah 43:18-19, 21-22, 24-25 In our repentance, the Lord remembers not our offenses.

Psalm 41 Lord, heal my soul, for I have sinned against you.

2 Corinthians 1:18-22 The Lord has set his seal upon us and given us the Holy Spirit.

Mark 2:1-12 Jesus has been given authority to forgive sins.

CATECHISM:

+ **1502** Jesus fulfills the prophetic promise: God will pardon offenses and heal illness.
+ **1511-1523** The nature and effects of sacramental anointing.
+ **1421, 1441** Jesus our physician. Only God forgives sin.
+ **1450-1454** Contrition and the penitent.
+ **1274, 1296** God's seal upon us.
+ **1065** Christ is the definitive "Amen" of the Father's love for us.

EIGHTH SUNDAY OF ORDINARY TIME (8Ob)

READING:

Hosea 2:16-17, 21-22 You shall know the Lord in justice, love, and mercy.

Psalm 103 The Lord is kind and merciful.

2 Corinthians 3:1-6 God has qualified us as ministers of the New Covenant.

Mark 2:18-22 Christ is the bridegroom and has promised to come again.

CATECHISM:

✝ **218-221** God's love for us.
✝ **1601-1605** Marriage in God's plan.
✝ **1638-1651** Faithfulness in married love.
✝ **772-773, 796** Church in nuptial union with Christ.
✝ **2786-2787** The gift of belonging to the Father in covenant.

NINTH SUNDAY OF
ORDINARY TIME (90*b*)

READING:

Deuteronomy 5:12-15 Keep the Sabbath holy. No working. You were once slaves.

Psalm 81 Sing with joy to God our help.

2 Corinthians 4:6-11 Earthen vessels.

Mark 2:23-3:6 Sabbath was made for man.

CATECHISM:

+ **345-349** Sabbath and Eighth Day.
+ **2168-2188, 2042** The centrality and importance of the Lord's Day. Church precept about Eucharistic participation on Sunday.
+ **1145-1152, 1166-1167** Celebrating the Church's liturgy.
+ **2685-2691** Fostering prayer: people and places that nourish the life of prayer.

TENTH SUNDAY OF ORDINARY TIME (10Ob)

READING:

Genesis 3:9-15 Enmity between serpent and the offspring of Eve.

Psalm 130 With the Lord there is mercy, and fullness of redemption.

2 Corinthians 4:13-5:1 We believe, therefore we speak.

Mark 3:20-35 Power over Satan. Blaspheming against the Spirit. "My kin are those who do God's will."

CATECHISM:

+ **337-344, 374-379, 385-400** Creation, Paradise, Fall. Satan's power. The first sin.
+ **410-412** Protoevangelium.
+ **547-550, 1673** Jesus' signs and exorcisms. Accusation that he works with demonic powers. Church exorcisms.
+ **1846-1869 (esp. 1864)** Mercy and sin. Sin against the Holy Spirit.

ELEVENTH SUNDAY OF ORDINARY TIME (11Ob)

READING:

Ezekiel 17:22-24 God will make the small tree great.

Psalm 92 Lord, it is good to give thanks to you.

2 Corinthians 5:6-10 We walk by faith. Our aim is to please Christ.

Mark 4:26-34 Parable of the mustard seed.

CATECHISM:

+ **279-289** Teaching about creation. Foundational for faith. Response to human concerns and investigations.
+ **788-795** Church and the kingdom of God.
+ **163-175** Faith the beginning of eternal life. Language of faith. Only one faith.
+ **748-757** Believing in the Catholic Church. Names and images of the Church.

TWELFTH SUNDAY OF ORDINARY TIME (120b)

READING:

Job 38:1-8, 11 The Lord is majestic, with power over creation.

Psalm 107 Give thanks to the Lord. His love is everlasting.

2 Corinthians 5:14-17 In Christ we are a new creation.

Mark 4:35-41 Jesus calms the storm. Disciples lack faith.

CATECHISM:

+ **290-314** Creation: its wonder and mystery. God's providence. The scandal of evil.
+ **160-162** Freedom of, necessity of, and perseverance in the faith.
+ **514-515, 547-548** Meaning of Christ's miracles.
+ **2415** Stewardship of creation.

THIRTEENTH SUNDAY OF ORDINARY TIME (13Ob)

READING:

Wisdom 1:13-15, 23-24 God did not make death.

Psalm 30 I will praise you, Lord, for you have rescued me.

2 Corinthians 8:7, 9:13-15 Become rich in love as in faith. Christ became poor for your sake.

Mark 5:21-43 (or shorter) Daughter of Jairus. Woman with hemorrhage.

CATECHISM:

+ **1877-1899** Love and the social dimension of Christian morality. Duty of each to care for all.
+ **356, 362-368, 391** God makes human beings in divine image, to be imperishable. The trap of death arises through devil's envy.
+ **1351** Collection for the poor as part of Mass in imitation of Christ.
+ **2407** Virtue of solidarity in justice.
+ **2616** Jesus answers prayer.
+ **1008-1014, 1020** Death transformed by Christ.

FOURTEENTH SUNDAY OF ORDINARY TIME (14Ob)

READING:

Ezekiel 2:2-5 I send you to rebels. Speak: They will know a prophet came.

Psalm 123 Our eyes are fixed on the Lord, pleading for his mercy.

2 Corinthians 12:7-10 My grace sufficient for you. Power seen in weakness.

Mark 5:1-16 Where did he get all this? No prophet is accepted in own country.

CATECHISM:

+ **1905-1917** The "common good." Participation in social life and taking personal responsibility for social concerns.
+ **268-274** God's almighty power is manifest in mercy and apparent powerlessness.
+ **851-856** Mission: at the heart of the Church even despite our human weakness.
+ **1808** Fortitude: firmness in difficult times.
+ **2581** Role of the prophet.

FIFTEENTH SUNDAY OF ORDINARY TIME (15Ob)

READING:

Amos 7:12-15 Off! This is king's sanctuary. I was no prophet, but Lord!

Psalm 85 Lord, let us see your kindness, and grant us your salvation.

Ephesians 1:3-14 (or shorter) God chose us in Christ: in him, he has given.

Mark 9:7-13 The twelve are sent, two by two. Take nothing! Shake dust.

CATECHISM:

+ **1928-1942** Social justice and persons. Solidarity. Equal rights despite personal differences.
+ **257, 600, 2012-2014, 2822-2824** God's plan of loving kindness. Predestination. "Thy will be done!"
+ **1077-1083** The Father: source of all blessing.
+ **857-865** Mission of the apostles and the apostolic nature of the Church.
+ **2807-2808** We "hallow" the name of God who calls us to be holy.

SIXTEENTH SUNDAY OF ORDINARY TIME (16Ob)

READING:

Jeremiah 23:1-6 Woe to bad shepherds. I myself will gather my people.

Psalm 23 The Lord is my shepherd; there is nothing I shall want.

Ephesians 2:13-18 Christ's peace, uniting Jews, Gentiles. Access together.

Mark 6:30-34 Apostles return. "Come apart!" The crowd, like sheep without a shepherd, followed.

CATECHISM:

+ **301-305** God's personal care for creation.
+ **360, 775, 820-822** Unity of the human race. The Church as sacrament of unity. The continuing call to unity.
+ **2401-2418** Social teaching of Church. Justice. Works of mercy and love for the poor.
+ **2302-2306** Christ is our peace. Safeguarding peace.
+ **2493-2499** Caring for the well-being of all. The importance of truthful and just social communications.

SEVENTEENTH SUNDAY OF ORDINARY TIME (17Ob)

READING:

2 Kings 4:42-44 Elisha gave the twenty loaves to one hundred men — with some left over!

Psalm 145 The hand of the Lord feeds us. He answers all our needs.

Ephesians 4:1-6 Live a worthy life! Unity. Peace from Spirit. One Lord, one faith, and one baptism.

John 6:1-15 Five thousand men. A few loaves. Jesus blessed and gave them out. Twelve baskets left.

CATECHISM:

+ **1200-1206** Unity of the Paschal mystery, yet diversity of liturgical forms.
+ **547-549** Signs of the kingdom of God.
+ **1333-1335** Eucharist. Bread and wine. Passover roots. Multiplication of loaves.
+ **1345-1354** Eucharistic action of the Church through the ages (structure of the Mass).
+ **1633-1637** Challenge to maintain unity in families of mixed marriages.

EIGHTEENTH SUNDAY OF ORDINARY TIME (18Ob)

READING:

Exodus 16:2-4, 12-15 Israel grumbles. Through Moses the Lord sends quail, then manna.

Psalm 78 The Lord gave them bread from heaven.

Ephesians 4:17, 20-24 No longer pagan! Live new life in Jesus. Put on new self.

John 6:24-35 Work not for perishable food, but for food of eternal life. I am the bread of life. Come to me and never hunger or thirst.

CATECHISM:

+ **606-611** Christ embraces the saving will of the Father, expressing in the Last Supper the gift of himself for the world.
+ **1333-1344** Institution of Eucharist. Jesus calls himself the bread of life and commands his followers to "do this."
+ **1402-1405** Eucharist: pledge of future glory.
+ **2042** Yearly communion (Church precept).
+ **1265-1266, 1694-1696** Called to live the new life in Christ.

NINETEENTH SUNDAY OF ORDINARY TIME (19Ob)

READING:

1 Kings 19:4-8 Elijah, wearied, slept, ate, drank, then walked forty days in strength of that bread to mountain of God.

Psalm 34 Taste and see the goodness of the Lord.

Ephesians 4:30-5:2 Do not sadden the Spirit. Cast evil aside. Forgive as dear children.

John 6:41-51 They murmured, "Bread from heaven?" No one comes unless drawn by Father. Eat this bread and live forever.

CATECHISM:

> ✝ **1355-1372** Eucharist: bread of heaven for the life of the world. Thanksgiving to the Father, sacrificial memorial of Christ and the Church.
> ✝ **1427-1429, 2581-2584** Elijah, the prophets, and conversion of the heart.
> ✝ **259** Work of the Father: drawing us to Christ.
> ✝ **2302-2306** Turning from anger toward peace.

TWENTIETH SUNDAY OF ORDINARY TIME (20Ob)

READING:

Proverbs 9:1-6 Wisdom: come, eat, drink my wine; forsake foolishness.

Psalm 34 Taste and see the goodness of the Lord.

Ephesians 5:15-20 Live wisely. Days are evil. Understand the Lord's will. Sing and give thanks.

John 6:51-58 How can he give his flesh to eat? My flesh is true food and drink.

CATECHISM:

✝ **1020, 1405, 1524, 2828-2837** Our "daily" bread. Medicine of immortality. Food for our "passing over" (viaticum).

✝ **1156-1158** Singing and music in the liturgical tradition.

✝ **1174-1178** Liturgy of the Hours: giving thanks always.

✝ **1373-1381** The Eucharist: Christ's true presence.

✝ **2585-2589** Psalms: prayer of God's people.

✝ **2639-2643** Prayer of praise in the Eucharist.

✝ **2826-2827** Prayer and God's will.

TWENTY-FIRST SUNDAY OF ORDINARY TIME (21Ob)

READING:

Joshua 24:1-2, 15-17, 18 Decide whom you serve. My family chooses the Lord. We, too!

Psalm 34 Taste and see the goodness of the Lord.

Ephesians 5:21-32 Be subordinate to one another — with husbands and wives as with Christ and the Church.

John 6:60-69 Disciples: hard saying! They left. The twelve remain: "To whom shall we go? You have the words of eternal life."

CATECHISM:

+ **757, 766** Church: spouse of the Lamb. Born of Christ's self-giving.
+ **772-776** Church: union with God and sacrament of salvation.
+ **1336, 1382-1401** Christ's offer of himself as food to eat. A "hard saying." The communion banquet and its fruits.
+ **2084-86, 2110-2114** God alone shall you serve. Human unity rooted in worship of the one God (First Commandment).

TWENTY-SECOND SUNDAY OF ORDINARY TIME (22Ob)

READING:

Deuteronomy 4:1-2, 6-8 Observe these statutes, that you may live. And enter the land. The Lord our God is so close to us. So wise are his ways.

Psalm 15 The one who does justice will live in the presence of the Lord.

James 1:17-18, 21-22, 27 Every good gift from Father. Welcome the Word. Care for orphans and widows.

Mark 7:1-8, 14-15, 21-23 Clean hands and unclean hearts. Not what enters a man but what comes from his heart makes him unclean.

CATECHISM:

+ **80-90** Scripture and tradition.
+ **574-582** Jesus and Israel. Jesus and the Law.
+ **212-214** God alone "is."
+ **2101-2109** Honoring God. Religion, vows, religious freedom (First Commandment).
+ **2337-2350** Vocation of personal integrity. Chastity (Sixth Commandment).

TWENTY-THIRD SUNDAY OF ORDINARY TIME (23Ob)

READING:

Isaiah 35:4-7 Fear not! God comes to save you – with healing.

Psalm 146 Praise the Lord, my soul!

James 2:1-5 No favoritism when rich or poor enter the assembly. God chose the poor.

Mark 7:31-37 Deaf man: Jesus touched ears, tongue: "Be opened!" "He has done all well."

CATECHISM:

> + **739-741** The Holy Spirit: source of Church's healing and sanctifying mission.
> + **1151-1152** Signs taken up by Christ and sacramental signs.
> + **1502-1505** The sick person before God. Christ the Physician.
> + **1929-1942, 2419-2425** Catholic social teaching. Respect for the person. Equality, differences, and solidarity.

TWENTY-FOURTH SUNDAY OF ORDINARY TIME (24Ob)

READING:

Isaiah 50:4-9 My face I did not shield from buffets. God is my help.

Psalm 116 I will walk before the Lord in the land of the living.

James 2:14-18 Useless to say to poor, "Keep well fed." Faith and works.

Mark 8:27-39 Who do they (and you) say I am? "The Christ!" Son of Man must suffer. Peter's rebuke. Take up the cross to follow.

CATECHISM:

+ **713-716** Suffering servant. The "poor" achieve the Holy Spirit's hidden mission.
+ **2443-2449** Works of mercy and love for the poor.
+ **1989-1996, 2006-2011** Justification. Human "merit" and God's grace.
+ **2544-2547** Poverty of the heart.
+ **440, 571-572, 601** Jesus, God's servant, suffers and dies for our redemption.
+ **471-474** Christ's soul and human knowledge.

TWENTY-FIFTH SUNDAY OF ORDINARY TIME (25Ob)

READING:

Wisdom 2:12, 17-20 The Just One is obnoxious to us. Let us condemn him to a shameful death. God will save him, if he is his Son.

Psalm 54 The Lord upholds my life.

James 3:16-4:3 Jealousy brings strife: Wisdom is peaceable. The fruit of righteousness. The roots of evil.

Mark 9:30-37 Son of Man is to be handed over. But disciples argued about who is greatest. To rank first, you must serve all.

CATECHISM:

+ **599-605** Christ's humble acceptance of death and God's plan of redeeming love.
+ **615-618** Jesus' obedience and our participation in his sacrifice.
+ **786, 1723** To reign with Christ we must serve like him.
+ **2535-2540** The upset caused by greed and envy.
+ **2735-2737** Complaining when our prayer is not heard.

TWENTY-SIXTH SUNDAY OF ORDINARY TIME (26Ob)

READING:

Numbers 11:25-29 Spirit bestowed on seventy elders. Two absent ones also prophesied. Complaints. "Would that all were prophets!"

Psalm 19 The precepts of the Lord give joy to the heart.

James 5:1-6 Wail, you rich, unjust ones. Wanton luxury rots away. You have killed the just.

Mark 9:38-43, 45, 47-48 A stranger worked miracles in your name! But whoever is not against us is for us. If your hand causes you to sin, cut it off.

CATECHISM:

+ **1033-1037** Hell.
+ **2422-2425, 2434, 2443-2449** Justice for workers. Love for the poor.
+ **2268-2269** Unjustified killing.
+ **2284-2287** Respect for the souls of others. Scandal.

TWENTY-SEVENTH SUNDAY OF ORDINARY TIME (27Ob)

READING:

Genesis 2:18-24 "Not good for man to be alone." Sleep. From Adam's rib God made a woman. Joy of Adam. Hence the two become one flesh.

Psalm 128 May the Lord bless us all the days of our lives.

Hebrews 2:9-11 Jesus rightly made perfect in suffering for "brothers."

Mark 10:2-16 (or shorter) Divorce? Not so in the beginning. Let no one separate what God has joined. Let the children come to me! Accept the kingdom like a child.

CATECHISM:

+ **369-373, 2360-2379** Man and woman: equality and difference. The love of husband and wife. Sexuality, fidelity, fruitfulness.
+ **2380-2391** Marriage undermined. Adultery and divorce.

TWENTY-EIGHTH SUNDAY OF ORDINARY TIME (28Ob)

READING:

Wisdom 7:7-11 Wisdom: better than gold, gems. All good comes with her.

Psalm 90 Fill us with your love, O Lord, and we will sing for joy!

Hebrews 4:12-13 Word of God living, effective. All bare to God's eyes.

Mark 10:17-30 How to gain eternal life? Follow commandments — then give all and follow me. "It is easier for a camel." Give for my sake and gain a hundredfold.

CATECHISM:

✛ **101-108, 131-133** Dignity of God's Word. Its place in life of the Church.
✛ **1854-1863** Gravity of sin. Mortal and venial.
✛ **1949-1960** Moral law. Natural moral law.
✛ **2652-2654** Prayerful reading of the Word of God.
✛ **2726-2728** Human objections and obstacles to prayer.
✛ **2052-2063** The Commandments. Their biblical tradition.

TWENTY-NINTH SUNDAY OF ORDINARY TIME (29Ob)

READING:

Isaiah 53:10-11 The Lord crushed him. He gives himself as offering for sin, bearing guilt of others.

Psalm 33 Lord, let your mercy be on us, as we place our trust in you.

Hebrews 4:14-16 Jesus: our great priest, tested as we are. Let us confidently approach the throne of grace.

Mark 10:35-45 (or 42-45) "Let us sit on your right and left!" "Can you drink my cup?" But the greatest will be the servant — like the Son of Man, a ransom for the many.

CATECHISM:

+ **536-537, 618** Christ's Passion: the baptism of pain. Our participation.
+ **599-609** Christ: handed over to suffering as he embraces the Father's loving will.
+ **440, 786** "Not to be served but to serve."
+ **2602** Jesus includes all in his prayer.
+ **2777-2778** Our worthiness in prayer.

THIRTIETH SUNDAY OF ORDINARY TIME (30Ob)

READING:

Jeremiah 31:7-9 Back from captivity. The blind and the lame. I will console them.

Psalm 126 The Lord has done great things for us. We are filled with joy.

Hebrews 5:1-6 High priest: called by God to offer sacrifices for self and others. So Christ was called, "You are my son . . . a priest forever."

Mark 10:46-52 Blind Bartimaeus: "Have pity! I want to see." "Your faith has healed you."

CATECHISM:

+ **541-550** The signs and wonders of Jesus manifest the welcome and restoration of the kingdom.
+ **2665-2669** Prayer to Jesus.
+ **783, 893, 901, 1141, 1537-1553** The priesthood of Christ. Priesthood in the Old Covenant and in the Church.

THIRTY-FIRST SUNDAY OF ORDINARY TIME (31Ob)

READING:

Deuteronomy 6:2-6 Keep Commandments and have long life in the land. The Lord alone is God. Love with whole heart.

Psalm 18 I love you, Lord, my strength.

Hebrews 7:23-28 Jesus remains forever with a priesthood that does not pass away – perfect forever.

Mark 12:28-34 Which command is greatest? Love God with all heart and soul, and your neighbor as yourself.

CATECHISM:

+ **199-202, 222-227** Believing in the one God.
+ **836-845** The one God's offer of salvation through the Church: relationships with other faiths.
+ **1362-1367** The sacrificial meal of Christ and of his Body, the Church.
+ **2083-2094** First: Love God. Faith, hope, and charity in relation to our worship of the one God.
+ **2196** Love of neighbor and God.

THIRTY-SECOND SUNDAY OF ORDINARY TIME (32Ob)

READING:

1 Kings 17:10-16 Elijah to widow: "Give me food." With last of her flour and oil she made him a meal. Her flour and oil did not run out.

Psalm 146 Praise the Lord, my soul!

Hebrews 9:24-28 Christ entered true sanctuary. He was offered once for all to take away sins of many. He comes a second time to bring salvation.

Mark 12:38-44 Beware scribes who seek honors. Observe the widow. She gave more than all the rest.

CATECHISM:

+ **1023-1029** Heaven.
+ **2544-2547** Call to detachment from riches. Example of the widow who gives from her poverty.
+ **2738-2741** Connecting our prayer with Jesus'.
+ **2849-2854** Victory of prayer over temptation and evil.

THIRTY-THIRD SUNDAY OF ORDINARY TIME (33Ob)

READING:

Daniel 12:1-3 Michael shall arise. Distress. Some rise to life, others to horror. The wise and just shine brightly.

Psalm 16 You are my inheritance, O Lord.

Hebrews 10:11-14, 18 Unlike the former sacrifices, Christ's one sacrifice has forever brought perfection.

Mark 13:24-32 Distress in skies: Son of Man comes, gathering his elect. Learn from the fig tree. Heaven and earth will pass, but my Word will not pass.

CATECHISM:

+ **1033-1037** Hell. Understanding this in light of God's love.
+ **1040-1050** Last Judgment. Call to conversion. Hope of new heaven and earth.
+ **1680-1690, 1010-1014** Funerals, prayers for the dead. Happy death.
+ **992-998** Progressive revelation of the Resurrection.

CHRIST THE KING

READING:

Daniel 7:13-14 A Son of Man comes. Receives everlasting dominion.

Psalm 93 The Lord is king; he is robed in majesty.

Revelation 1:5-8 To Jesus: glory forever. Every eye shall see. Even those who pierced him. Alpha and Omega.

John 18:33-37 "Are you the King?" "Not from the world ... For this I have come into the world — to bear witness to the truth."

CATECHISM:

+ **1042-1050** New heavens and new earth. The final kingdom of Christ the King.
+ **160** The freedom of faith. Christ witnesses to truth and does not impose it.
+ **668-672** Christ's reign, through the Church and yet to come.

TRANSFIGURATION OF THE LORD (AUGUST 6)

READING:

Daniel 7:9-10, 13-14 Ancient one. Myriads attended. Son of Man given rule.

Psalm 97 The Lord is king, the most high over all the earth.

2 Peter 1:16-19 Not myths. We ourselves heard, saw his splendor.

Mark 9:2-10 "This is my beloved Son. Listen to him."

CATECHISM:

+ **554-556** Transfiguration — a foretaste of the kingdom.
+ **422-424, 606-608** The whole life of the Beloved Son among us is an offering to the Father.
+ **660-664** The glory and dominion of the Risen One at the Father's right hand.
+ **2794-2796** The majesty of the Father who is "in heaven."
+ **2583** Moses and Elijah: finding God in varied ways, now they see the unveiled face of Christ.

ASSUMPTION OF THE BLESSED VIRGIN

READING:

Revelation 11:19, 12:1-6, 10 Great sign: woman clothed with the sun. Her newborn child is saved from the devouring dragon.

Psalm 45 The queen stands at your right hand, arrayed in gold.

1 Corinthians 15:20-26 In Adam all die. In Christ all will come to life as he conquers every enemy, even death itself.

Luke 1:39-56 Visit to Elizabeth: "Blessed is she who believed." Magnificat.

CATECHISM:

> ✝ **1138** Celebrants of the heavenly liturgy.
> ✝ **410-412, 495, 655, 1008** Adam's death and Mary, the New Eve. Christ's Resurrection and the destiny of his Church.
> ✝ **668, 671-672** Christ reigns until all things are subjected to him. The distress of the Church as it waits.
> ✝ **717, 721-726** The Holy Spirit works in Mary, the New Eve.
> ✝ **273, 2617-2619** The prayer of the Virgin Mary.
> ✝ **964-970** Mary: united with Christ — also in her Assumption — is our Mother in the order of grace.

SOLEMNITY OF ALL SAINTS

READING:

Revelation 7:2-4, 9-14 A crowd that no one could number – they washed their robes in blood of Lamb.

Psalm 24 Lord, this is the people that longs to see your face.

1 John 3:1-3 The Father's love. We are God's children now. Then we will be like him.

Matthew 5:1-12 On the mountain, Jesus teaches the beatitudes.

CATECHISM:

+ **1138, 2642** The heavenly liturgy. Its celebrants. Its prayer of praise.
+ **1296** The "seal" of God's servants (confirmation).
+ **163-164** Faith: tasting in advance the beatific vision, even amid trials.
+ **1023-1024** Heaven: seeing God face-to-face. Communion of life and love with the Most Holy Trinity.
+ **1161** Mary and the saints. Participants in world's salvation and in communion with us (holy images).
+ **1716-1724** Our vocation to beatitude.
+ **520** Christ, our model of holiness.
+ **828-829, 946-948, 954-957, 1173** The Church is holy. The communion of saints. Memorials of the saints.
+ **1474-1477** Sharing the treasury of the communion of saints (relating to indulgences).
+ **2683-2684** The saints as examples of prayer.

+ *Cycle C*

FIRST SUNDAY OF ADVENT (1Ac)

READING:

Jeremiah 33:14-16 I will raise up a just shoot. They will call Jerusalem, "The Lord our justice."

Psalm 25 To you, O Lord, I lift my soul.

1 Thessalonians 3:12–4:2 May the Lord strengthen your hearts. Conduct yourselves to please God.

Luke 21:25-28, 34-36 Sign in the heavens. Fright on earth. The Son of Man will come with power. Let not your heart be drowsy, but stand erect.

CATECHISM:

+ **1021, 1038-1041** The Particular Judgment and the Last Judgment.
+ **675-679** The Church's final trial. Victory not by Church's historic triumph but by God's saving action. Christ as judge of living and dead.
+ **2612, 2849** Vigilance in prayer.

IMMACULATE CONCEPTION

READING:

Genesis 3:9-15, 20 After eating from the tree, Adam hid in fear. The woman reveals, "The serpent tricked me into it, so I ate it." God declared enmity between her offspring and the serpent's.

Psalm 98 Sing to the Lord a new song, for he has done marvelous deeds.

Ephesians 1:3-6, 11-12 God chose us before the foundation of the world to be holy and blameless.

Luke 1:26-38 The angel Gabriel announces to Mary: "Hail, full of grace!"

CATECHISM:

+ **971-972** Devotion to Mary. "All generations will call me blessed." Mary as icon of Church.
+ **490-494** The Immaculate Conception.
+ **2617-2619** The prayer of the Virgin Mary. Cooperation with God. Acceptance, "fiat," intercessor.

SECOND SUNDAY OF ADVENT (2Ac)

READING:

Baruch 5:1-9 Jerusalem, take off your mourning robe. Look, God is leading Israel in joy.

Psalm 126 The Lord has done great things for us. We are filled with joy.

Philippians 1:4-6, 8-11 May you be blameless right up to the day of Christ.

Luke 3:1-6 John: a herald's voice crying, "Make ready the way. All will see God's salvation."

CATECHISM:

+ **1877-1889** Human vocation to show forth the image of God. Its communal character. Society: conversion and society. Keeping first things first. Inner conversion.
+ **1905-1917** The common good. Responsibility and participation.
+ **2517-2527** Purity: in the heart, behavior, and society.

THIRD SUNDAY OF ADVENT (3Ac)

READING:

Zephaniah 3:14-18 The Lord will renew you in his love and rejoice over you with gladness.

(Psalm) Isaiah 12 Cry out with joy and gladness, for among you is the great and Holy One of Israel.

Philippians 4:4-7 Rejoice in the Lord always!

Luke 3:10-18 It is he whom John foretold; it is he who will baptize in the Holy Spirit.

CATECHISM:

+ **1691-1698** Dignity of Christian life. Incorporation into Christ by baptism. Temple of Holy Spirit. Walking the path that leads to life. Catechesis and "newness of life."
+ **1804-1811** Human virtues. "Cardinal" virtues of prudence, justice, fortitude, temperance — purified by God's grace.
+ **722, 2767** Mary's joy as the "Daughter of Zion."
+ **2629-2633** Petitionary prayer in every need (especially for the kingdom to come).

FOURTH SUNDAY OF ADVENT (4Ac)

READING:

Micah 5:1-4 From Bethlehem shall come the one who will rule Israel.

Psalm 80 Lord, make us turn to you. Let us see your face, and we shall be saved.

Hebrews 10:5-10 Christ will protect and save us, offering himself once and for all in doing the Father's will.

Luke 1:39-45 Elizabeth calls Mary "blessed," because of her faith and the obedience with which she bore Christ.

CATECHISM:

+ **495-507** Mary's virginity. Her virginal motherhood in God's plan.
+ **614** Christ's sacrifice fulfills all others.
+ **148-149** Mary: obedient in faith.
+ **2673-2679** Prayer in communion with the Mother of God ("Hail Mary").

THE NATIVITY OF THE LORD (CHRISTMAS)

READING:

Given the vast scope and great riches of the Scriptures proclaimed in the Nativity of the Lord, there is no attempt here to refer to particular passages. Instead, some overarching theological themes are offered.

CATECHISM:

+ **422-429** Good News: God has sent his Son. Inviting people of every era to enter the joy of communion with Christ (repeated from Christmas A). Incarnate Christ as heart of catechesis.

+ **50** Revelation: God comes to meet man. The plan fully revealed in Christ.

+ **456-463, 478** Why did the Word become flesh? The Incarnation. We are loved in the human heart of the Incarnate Word.

+ **525-526** The Christmas mystery.

THE HOLY FAMILY OF JESUS, MARY, AND JOSEPH

READING:

Sirach 3:2-6, 12-14 Father and mother are to be honored.

Psalm 128 Blessed are those who fear the Lord and walk in his ways.

Colossians 3:12-21 As God's chosen ones, live in harmony and thankfulness. **Or 1 Samuel 1:20-22, 24-28** Hannah presents her son Samuel for service to the Lord.

Psalm 84 Blessed are they who dwell in your house, O Lord.

1 John 3:1-2, 21-24 By the Father's love we are God's children now.

Luke 2:41-52 His parents found Jesus at the temple in the midst of the teachers.

CATECHISM:

+ **2221-2228** Duties of parents (repeated from Holy Family "A").
+ **532-534** The finding in the temple.
+ **1652-1654** Openness to fertility in reference to Hannah.
+ **2204-2206** Family as domestic Church.
+ **2232-2233** The family and the kingdom.

SOLEMNITY OF THE BLESSED VIRGIN MARY, MOTHER OF GOD

READING:

Numbers 6:22-27 The Lord's name was to be invoked upon the people in blessing: "The Lord bless you and keep you."

Psalm 67 May God bless us in his mercy.

Galatians 4:4-7 In the fullness of time, God sent his Son, born of a woman.

Luke 2:16-21 The shepherds went to Bethlehem and found Mary and Joseph and the infant lying in the manger. Mary reflected on all these things in her heart.

CATECHISM:

+ **967-970** Mary: our mother in order of grace.
+ **2599** Jesus learned to pray in his human heart. The witness of his mother who treasured God's deeds in her heart.
+ **495** Mary's divine motherhood.
+ **1667-1672** The call to "be a blessing" and "to bless" (sacramentals).

EPIPHANY

READING:

Isaiah 60:1-6 Rise up in splendor. The glory of the Lord shines upon you.

Psalm 72 Lord, every nation on earth will adore you.

Ephesians 3:2-3, 5-6 The mystery made known. The Gentiles are coheirs of the promise.

Matthew 2:1-12 Magi from the East arrived. "We saw his star." Finding the child, they offered their gifts.

CATECHISM:

+ **528-529** The mystery of Epiphany. Presentation in temple reveals Jesus as "light to the nations."
+ **515-519** Gospels written to share faith with others. Whole life of Jesus is Father's revelation. Christ's riches are everybody's property.
+ **124** The Word of God. God's saving power for everyone who has faith.
+ **27-43** Ways of coming to know God (created world, human person, intellect). Knowledge of God according to the Church. How can we speak about God?
+ **360-361** Human race as a unity born of our common origin as God's creation. Human solidarity and charity.

BAPTISM OF THE LORD

READING:

Isaiah 42:1-4, 6-7 Here is my servant, called for the victory of justice.

Psalm 29 The Lord will bless his people with peace.

Acts 10:34-38 God shows no partiality. He proclaimed peace through Jesus Christ, beginning after John's baptism, when Jesus was anointed with the Holy Spirit.

Luke 3:15-16, 21-22 After Jesus was baptized and was praying, heaven was opened and the Holy Spirit descended upon him.

CATECHISM:

+ **50** God wills to reveal himself. Christ as God's perfect revelation.
+ **65** God has said everything in his Word, his Son.
+ **150-152** The response of faith. To believe in God alone, in his Son, in the Holy Spirit.
+ **438** Jesus' messianic consecration for mission.
+ **535-537** The mystery of the baptism of Jesus.
+ **727** Son and Spirit together in mission.
+ **1217-1225** Prefigurations of baptism in Old Covenant.

FIRST SUNDAY OF LENT (1Lc)

READING:

Deuteronomy 26:4-10 Moses recounts the great events of salvation history.

Psalm 91 Be with me, Lord, when I am in trouble.

Romans 10:8-13 We confess Jesus to be Lord, for God raised him from the dead.

Luke 4:1-13 Jesus is ever faithful, resisting temptation to forsake his Father's mission.

CATECHISM:

+ **1846-1853** Mercy and sin. Kinds of sin.
+ **2012-2016, 2558** Christian call to holiness. Call to the life of prayer. A living relationship with the true God.
+ **2119** Adoring only God. Tempting God.
+ **430-432, 441-451** Titles of Jesus as Savior, Son of God, and Lord.
+ **538-540** Temptations of Jesus.
+ **2095-2098** Adoration: acknowledging God as ultimate source, not turning in on oneself.

SECOND SUNDAY OF LENT (2Lc)

READING:

Genesis 15:5-12, 17-18 God seals the covenant with Abram.

Psalm 27 The Lord is my light and my salvation.

Philippians 3:17–4:1 or 3:20–4:1 Our lowly bodies will be changed to conform with his glorified body.

Luke 9:28-36 Going up to the mountain to pray, Jesus is transfigured before Peter, James, and John.

CATECHISM:

+ **59-61** Call of Abraham.
+ **557-558** The ascent to Jerusalem.
+ **554-556, 697** Transfiguration. Cloud as image of Holy Spirit.
+ **2600** Jesus' prayer.
+ **999, 1003** Our lowly bodies to become like his glorified body.
+ **2581-2584** Elijah and Moses took the desert road to encounter the mysterious presence of God. Now they see the unveiled face of Christ.

THIRD SUNDAY OF LENT (3Lc)

READING:

Exodus 3:1-8, 13-15 Moses encounters God in the burning bush. When the Israelites ask my name tell them, "I AM sent me to you."

Psalm 103 The Lord is kind and merciful.

1 Corinthians 10:1-6, 10-12 Do not be self-righteous; heed God's call.

Luke 13:1-9 The parable of the fig tree speaks of the urgency of the call to conversion.

CATECHISM:

+ **203-209, 2142-2145, 2574-2577, 2777** Revelation of God's name. The burning bush. Moses' prayer. We dare to pray in Christ.
+ **1691-1698** Life in Christ ("fruitfulness").
+ **1093-1096** In the Spirit, the Old Covenant prefigures the New.
+ **1122-1124** Sacraments: rooted in faith.

FOURTH SUNDAY OF LENT (4Lc)

READING:

Joshua 5:9, 10-12 Now in the Promised Land, God's people kept the Passover and could eat of the fruit of the land.

Psalm 34 Taste and see the goodness of the Lord.

2 Corinthians 5:17-21 In Christ: a new creation. Christ ministered God's reconciliation — a ministry now given over to the Church.

Luke 15:1-3, 11-32 Your brother was lost. He has been found. He was dead and has come back to life (the prodigal).

CATECHISM:

+ **545** Jesus invited sinners to table of the kingdom.
+ **588-589** Scandal of Jesus' sharing with sinners and identifying God's attitude with his merciful conduct.
+ **604-605** God's initiative of universal redeeming love.
+ **981-983** Christ commissioned the Church to carry out the ministry of reconciliation.
+ **1430-1433** Interior penance.
+ **1465-1467** Priest as instrument of Christ's mercy and welcome in sacramental penance.
+ **2839** Humble confidence of a sinner before God.
+ **1439** Process of conversion like that of prodigal son.
+ **2794-2795** Heaven: The Father's house, from which sin exiles us and to which conversion of heart enables us to return.

FIFTH SUNDAY OF LENT (5Lc)

READING:

Isaiah 43:16-21 God does a new thing. A way in the desert and rivers in the wasteland.

Psalm 126 The Lord has done great things for us. We are filled with joy.

Philippians 3:8-14 I forfeit all in order to find my wealth in Christ.

John 8:1-11 The woman caught in adultery. "Let the one without sin cast a stone."

CATECHISM:

+ **1468-1470** Effects of sacramental penance.
+ **426-428, 2653-2654** Christ-centered catechesis. Losing all in order to know Christ. Prayerful encounter with Scripture.
+ **827** The holy Church is composed of sinful people. All members must acknowledge this.
+ **1265-1266** New creature through baptism.
+ **1854-1863** Gravity of sin (mortal and venial).

PASSION SUNDAY

PROCESSION:

Luke 19:28-40

READING:

Isaiah 50:4-7 I gave my back to those who beat me. The Lord is my help. I have set my face like flint, knowing that I shall not be put to shame.

Psalm 22 My God, my God, why have you abandoned me?

Philippians 2:6-11 Christ humbled himself, obedient even to death on a cross. God greatly exalted him.

Luke 22:14-23, 56 or 23:1-49 The Passion of our Lord Jesus Christ.

CATECHISM:

+ **595-598** All sinners cause Christ's Passion. Jewish people not collectively responsible.
+ **1850-1851** Sin as offense against God — overcome in Passion of Christ.
+ **557-560** Jesus' entry into Jerusalem.
+ **449, 612, 713** Jesus: "in the form of God," "obedient unto death" and "servant."
+ **2605-2606** The compassion of Christ on the cross embraces all humanity's troubles.

HOLY THURSDAY EVENING MASS OF THE LORD'S SUPPER

READING:

Exodus 12:1-8, 11-14 The Israelites prepared and shared the sacrificial lamb — like those who are in flight. "It is the Passover of the Lord."

Psalm 116 Our blessing-cup is a communion with the Blood of Christ.

1 Corinthians 11:23-26 As often as you eat this bread and drink the cup, you proclaim the death of the Lord until he comes.

John 13:1-15 The hour has come. Jesus loved them to the end. "I have given you a model. . . . As I have done for you, you should also do."

CATECHISM:

> **Glory in the cross of Christ**
> + **606-607** Christ freely embraces the will of his Father.
> + **608-609** The Lamb of God loves his own to the end.
> + **610-611** At supper with his friends, Christ anticipates the free offering of his life.
> + **612** The sacrificial cup of Gethsemane.
> + **613-614** The sacrificial death of the Lamb of God.
> + **615-618** Christ's obedience even to death, loving his own to the end. Our share in his sacrifice.
> + **440, 520, 786** The "Christ," our model. His royalty revealed in service.

+ **2746-2750** Christ's prayer when "the hour" had come.

The Eucharist instituted

+ **1322-1327** The perpetuation of the sacrifice of the cross. Completes our initiation into Christ.

+ **1334, 1337-1344** The Holy Eucharist. Rooted in the Passover event and Christ's own Passover. Done in memory of him "until he comes."

+ **1356-1368** The Church carries out the Lord's command, offering the sacrifice of praise to the Father and the memorial of Christ's Passover.

+ **1380-1381** The event of his Passion: facing his departure in bodily form. Christ gives the sacrament of his true presence.

+ **1382-1384, 1403** Eating and drinking the Paschal banquet. Awaiting its fulfillment in God's kingdom.

The Priesthood of Christ continues in his Church

+ **1544-1545** Christ, true and only priest of the New Covenant, offers his redemptive sacrifice on the cross.

+ **1546-1548** Christ's priesthood continues in the community of believers and, uniquely, in the ministerial priesthood.

+ **1066-1068** The work of salvation, principally in the Paschal mystery, is manifest in the liturgy.

+ **1085, 1088-1089** Christ is active in the liturgy, associating the Church with himself in making present his Paschal mystery.

GOOD FRIDAY OF THE LORD'S PASSION

READING:

Isaiah 52:13–53:12 God's servant. Wounded for our sins, carrying the guilt of all.

Psalm 31 Father, into your hands I commend my spirit.

Hebrews 4:14-16, 5:7-9 Jesus, the great high priest, tested in every way, yet without sin. He learned obedience from what he suffered and became the source of eternal salvation.

John 18:1–19:42 The Passion of our Lord Jesus Christ.

CATECHISM:

+ **711-716, 1505** Christ: God's servant, taking the form of a slave yet anointed in the Spirit to bring freedom, healing, and peace to the poor.
+ **595-598** The trial of Jesus. Responsibility for his death.
+ **599-600** Christ's violent death. Not outside the plan of God.
+ **601-603** Christ, the sinless one, suffers for our sins.
+ **604-605** God takes the initiative in redeeming love.
+ **1992, 2305** Justification by the cross of Christ. Christ makes peace on the cross.
+ **766** The Church is born of Christ's total self-giving, coming forth from his side as he died on the cross.

EASTER VIGIL

READING:

Given the vast scope and great riches of the Scriptures proclaimed in the Great Vigil, there is no attempt here to refer to particular passages. Instead, some overarching theological themes of this night are offered.

CATECHISM:

+ **142, 260, 460** God's fundamental purpose: the entrance of his creatures into the perfect communion of the Holy Trinity.

+ **290-301** Creation: work of the Trinity, for God's glory, upheld by God.

+ **355-361** Humanity: image of God. Restored in the New Adam.

+ **396-404, 412** Sin brings death into human history. "O happy fault."

+ **603-605, 2572** God manifests benevolent, all-embracing love as he gives his beloved Son (prefigured in the sacrifice of Isaac).

+ **624-628** Christ in the tomb. Our baptismal union with him there.

+ **272, 638, 647, 654** Resurrection: God's power in apparent powerlessness. The crowning truth of our faith. The "truly blessed night." Its meaning for us.

+ **1214-1222, 1225** Baptism: plunging into Christ's death, regeneration, and enlightenment. Rooted in history of salvation and Christ's Passover.

+ **1262-1674** Baptism for the forgiveness of sins. A new creation. Incorporation into Christ. Union with other believers. Consecration for religious worship.

+ **1362-1364** Paschal "remembrance": Christ's Passover made present in the Eucharist.

+ **1612, 1617** Initiation into a nuptial union between God and his people.

+ **2560-2565** Prayer: Christ meets us at the well where we go in our thirst. Our covenant "from the heart." Our communion.

+ **62-64, 759-766** The formation of God's People in covenant. Expectation of renewal. Gathering the scattered children — the mystery of the Church revealed from creation to the cross.

EASTER SUNDAY

READING:

Acts 10:34, 37-43 Peter preaches: In the Holy Spirit, Jesus brought goodness and healing. They put him to death, but God raised him. We who ate and drank with him after he rose from the dead are his witnesses.

Psalm 118 This is the day the Lord has made; let us rejoice and be glad.

Colossians 3:1-4 Raised with Christ, seek what is above, where Christ is. **Or 1 Corinthians 5:6-8** Clear out the old yeast that you may become fresh dough. Christ, our Paschal lamb, has been sacrificed.

John 20:1-9 Mary went to the tomb and found it empty. Peter and John then came and saw the burial cloths, for Christ had to rise from the dead. Or (at afternoon or evening Masses) **Luke 24:13-35** The road to Emmaus. They recognized him in the breaking of bread.

CATECHISM:

+ **640-642** The empty tomb. The appearance to the holy women. The witness of the apostles in building the new era.
+ **185-191** The baptismal profession of faith.
+ **272** Resurrection as revelation of God's victory in face of apparent powerlessness.
+ **1002-1004** Already risen with Christ through baptism, we await the final resurrection.
+ **1168-1169** Easter Triduum as source of light for whole year. Easter as "feast of feasts."

When Luke's Emmaus Gospel is read:

+ **601** Christ's saving death was in accord with the Scriptures.
+ **1329, 1347** The Risen One reveals himself in the Eucharist.

SECOND SUNDAY OF EASTER (2Ec)

READING:

Acts 5:12-16 The apostles worked many signs, especially for the sick. Great numbers were added to them.

Psalm 118 Give thanks to the Lord for he is good. His love is everlasting.

Revelation 1:8-11, 12-13, 17-19 On the Lord's day John had a heavenly vision. Jesus told him not to be afraid, "I am the first and last; once I was dead but now I am alive forever."

John 20:19-31 The risen Lord meets with the disciples, shares the Holy Spirit. Thomas is absent and will not believe until he sees.

CATECHISM:

+ **153-165** Faith as grace. A human act. Faith and understanding.
+ **166-175** "We believe." The "faith of the Church." Formulations express the realities in which we believe. Only one faith.
+ **625-626** Christ's body lay in death in the tomb. His true Resurrection.
+ **999** The body of the risen Christ: pattern for our resurrected bodies.
+ **1507-1509** "Heal the sick": the care of the disciples for the sick as witness to risen Lord.
+ **1987-1995** Our justification, merited by the Passion of Christ and communicated through faith and baptism, is the greatest expression of God's mercy.

THIRD SUNDAY OF EASTER (3Ec)

READING:

Acts 5:27-32, 40-41 The apostles testify before the Sanhedrin, obeying God rather than men.

Psalm 30 I will praise you, Lord, for you have rescued me.

Revelation 5:11-14 Worthy is the Lamb that was slain to receive power. All in heaven worshiped.

John 21:1-19 (or 21:1-14) After a night of fruitless fishing, the apostles see the risen Jesus. At his Word they haul in many fish. He eats with them on the shore. Then to Simon: "Do you love me? Feed my lambs."

CATECHISM:

+ **553, 1428-1429** Peter's responsibility for Christ's flock. His repentance after denial of Christ.
+ **1166-1167** The "first day of the week." Day of assembly and celebration of the Resurrection.
+ **2639, 2642-2643** Praise, the purest prayer. The heavenly liturgy in praise of the Lamb. The Eucharist as complete form of prayer.
+ **2242** Obligation to disregard immoral directives of civil authorities.
+ **893-896** Bishops as shepherds of Christ's flock.

FOURTH SUNDAY OF EASTER (4Ec)

READING:

Acts 13:14, 43-52 Having spoken God's Word first to the Jews, Paul and Barnabas turn to the Gentiles.

Psalm 100 We are his people, the sheep of his flock.

Revelation 7:9, 14-17 The great heavenly multitude who washed their robes in the blood of the Lamb, who will shepherd them to the life-giving water.

John 10:27-30 My sheep hear my voice and follow me to eternal life. The Father has given them to me. The Father and I are one.

CATECHISM:

+ **74-76** God's saving self-communication through his Word.
+ **1137-1139** Celebrants of the heavenly liturgy.
+ **597-600** Christ handed over to death. Human responsibility and the plan of God.
+ **604-607** Christ's response to the Father's initiative of redeeming love.

FIFTH SUNDAY OF EASTER (5*Ec*)

READING:

Acts 14:21-27 In various towns Paul and Barnabas proclaim the Good News and encourage the disciples. They returned to Jerusalem and reported what God had done with them.

Psalm 145 I will praise your name forever, my king and my God.

Revelation 21:1-5 New heaven, new earth, new Jerusalem: God's dwelling with the human race. No more death. "I make all things new."

John 13:31-33, 34-35 The Son of Man is glorified. "I am with you only a little longer; love one another."

CATECHISM:

+ **1042-1046** Hope of the new heaven and new earth.
+ **1186** Liturgical celebration. Cross the threshold to "house of God."
+ **1823-1829** The new commandment of love.
+ **2842** Sharing God's loving mind. Forgiving those who sin against us.

SIXTH SUNDAY OF EASTER (6Ec)

READING:

Acts 15:1-2, 22-29 The Gentile converts and the Mosaic law. "It is the decision of the Holy Spirit and of us."

Psalm 67 O God, let all the nations praise you!

Revelation 21:10-14, 22-23 The heavenly Jerusalem: no temple, no sun — for God and the Lamb replace these things.

John 14:23-29 Love me, keep my word, and my Father and I will dwell with you. After I go away, the Advocate will teach you everything.

CATECHISM:

+ **260** Ultimate purpose of God: our entry into perfect unity of Blessed Trinity.
+ **243-244** The "Advocate" completes the revelation of the Father and the Son.
+ **788** Communion with Jesus: more intense with the sending of the Spirit.
+ **2615** Prayer in the Spirit: deeper participation in divine life.
+ **1099** Liturgical action of the Spirit: living memory of the Church.
+ **77-79** Living transmission of the Gospel through the Spirit in Church's tradition.
+ **888-892** Church abides in truth through the ministry of the Magisterium.

SOLEMNITY OF THE ASCENSION OF THE LORD

READING:

Acts 1:1-11 After appearing to them through forty days, the risen Christ was lifted up. They were to await the baptism with the Holy Spirit.

Psalm 47 God mounts his throne to shouts of joy. A blare of trumpets for the Lord.

Ephesians 1:17-23 May God's power work in you — the power that raised Christ from the dead, seated him at God's right hand and places all things under his feet. **Or Hebrews 9:24-28, 10:19-23** Christ, our great high priest, entered the heavenly sanctuary to offer the perfect sacrifice. Through his blood and in his flesh we have confident entrance into that sanctuary.

Luke 24:46-53 You are witnesses to Christ's death and Resurrection. You will be clothed with power from on high. Then Jesus was taken up to heaven.

CATECHISM:

+ **519, 662** The ascended Christ enters the heavenly sanctuary and remains our priestly advocate in the Father's presence.
+ **730, 735, 1287** Gift of the Spirit, power from on high and source of mission.
+ **1084-1090** Christ in glory is now at work in the liturgy.
+ **1127-1129** The power of God is the source of the effectiveness of the sacraments.

SEVENTH SUNDAY OF EASTER (7Ec)

READING:

Acts 7:55-60 Martyrdom of Stephen: "I see the Son of Man standing at God's right hand. . . . Lord, do not hold this sin against them."

Psalm 97 The Lord is king, the most high over all the earth.

Revelation 22:12-14, 16-17, 20 "I am coming soon." The Alpha and the Omega. The Spirit and the Bride say, "Come."

John 17:20-26 "I pray not just for them but for those who will believe in me through their word: that they may all be one. I wish them to be with me where I am."

CATECHISM:

+ **659, 671, 2635-2636** With Christ in glory, the Church gives self-sacrificing witness.
+ **260, 820** Basic purpose of God: union of creation with the Holy Trinity. The unity of the disciples.
+ **425-429** Catechesis: sharing with others our communion with Christ.
+ **796, 1130, 1403, 2548-2550, 2816-2821** Cry of the Spirit and the Bride: "Thy kingdom come!"

PENTECOST

VIGIL (CATECHISM):

2655-2658 Prayer: internalizes the liturgy and relies on faith, hope, and love.

READING:

Acts 2:1-11 They were all filled with the Holy Spirit and began to speak. All who heard them heard in their native language.

Psalm 104 Lord, send out your Spirit and renew the face of the earth.

1 Corinthians 12:3-7, 12-13 Different gifts, but the same Spirit. In one Spirit we were all baptized into one body, able to say "Jesus is Lord." **Or Romans 8:8-17** Live by the Spirit as sons of God, heirs with Christ who cry out "Abba, Father."

John 20:19-23 The risen Jesus meets his disciples: "Peace be with you. As the Father has sent me, I send you. Receive the Holy Spirit. Whose sins you forgive are forgiven them." Or **John 14:15-16, 23-26** Whoever loves me will keep my word. The Father and I will dwell with him, and the Father will give another Advocate to teach everything.

CATECHISM:

+ **691-701** Titles of the Holy Spirit.
+ **790-791, 798, 951, 1267, 1830-1832** Gifts and fruits of Holy Spirit. Unity of the one body.
+ **767-768, 2623-2625** Church: "gathered in prayer." Open to and gifted by the Holy Spirit.
+ **2670-2672** Holy Spirit, the Master of Prayer.
+ **1996-2005** Grace as Spirit-given participation in divine life.

SOLEMNITY OF THE MOST HOLY TRINITY

READING:

Proverbs 8:22-31 God's wisdom says: Before the earth was made, I was brought forth. God's craftsman and delight.

Psalm 8 O Lord, our God, how wonderful your name in all the earth!

Romans 5:1-5 Justified by faith, we have peace with God through Jesus Christ, in God's love poured out in the Holy Spirit.

John 16:12-15 Everything the Father has is mine. The Spirit will guide you to all truth by taking what is mine and declaring it to you.

CATECHISM:

+ **215-217** God is truth.
+ **243-246, 687** Spirit makes known the Word of the Father.
+ **2563-2565, 2615, 2664** Prayer: covenant and communion with the Holy Trinity.
+ **91-95** Spirit guides all the faithful in "sense of faith."
+ **465** Christ: of one substance with the Father.

SOLEMNITY OF THE MOST HOLY BODY AND BLOOD OF CHRIST

READING:

Genesis 14:18-20 Melchizedek, with bread and wine, blessed Abram and God Most High.

Psalm 110 You are a priest forever, in the line of Melchizedek.

1 Corinthians 11:23-26 I received from the Lord what I handed on to you about the supper on the night he was handed over. So, whenever you eat this bread and drink the cup, you proclaim the Lord's death.

Luke 9:11-17 Jesus took the loaves, spoke a blessing, broke them, and fed the five thousand. All were satisfied.

CATECHISM:

+ **1356-1381** The sacramental sacrifice.
+ **610-611, 1356-1358, 2042** The Last Supper: the supreme expression of his self-offering faithfully maintained by the Church in the Eucharist. Church precept about yearly Communion.
+ **1140-1144, 1544-1547** The priesthood of Christ continued in the Church.
+ **1333-1344** Signs of bread and wine in Old Covenant. Institution of Eucharist. Church's faithful action "until he comes."
+ **1130, 1402-1405, 2770-2772** Celebrating the Eucharist "until he comes."

SECOND SUNDAY OF ORDINARY TIME (20c)

READING:

Isaiah 62:1-5 You shall be called "espoused." As a bridegroom rejoices in his bride, so God will rejoice in you.

Psalm 96 Proclaim his marvelous deeds to all the nations.

1 Corinthians 12:4-11 Different gifts but the same Spirit.

John 2:1-11 The wedding at Cana.

CATECHISM:

+ **1612-1617** Marriage in the Lord.
+ **1601-1611** Marriage in God's plan, under the law and in the Lord.
+ **1621-1632** Celebration of marriage.
+ **2618** Mary's intercession and the Cana wedding.
+ **2331-2336, 2364-2365** Male and female: marital sexuality. Intimate partnership (fidelity) (Sixth Commandment).

THIRD SUNDAY OF
ORDINARY TIME (3Oc)

READING:

Nehemiah 8:2-4, 5-6, 8-10 Ezra read from the book of the law of God and the people answered, "Amen!"

Psalm 19 Your words, Lord, are spirit and life.

1 Corinthians 12:12-30 (or 12:12-14, 27) Many members, one body.

Luke 1:1-4, 4:14-21 I have compiled this narrative about Jesus. He began his public ministry by returning to Galilee: "The Spirit of the Lord is upon me."

CATECHISM:

+ **124-127** Formation of New Testament.
+ **541-550** Kingdom of God is at hand. Proclamation of the kingdom.
+ **1961** Old Law in Nehemiah.
+ **436, 695, 713-714, 763-764, 1286** Jesus, the Anointed One, inaugurates the Church by proclaiming the reign of God.
+ **1153-1155, 1348-1349** Sacramental words and actions. The gathering of the liturgical assembly for the Word of God.
+ **1200-1204** Unity in the diverse forms of liturgical celebration.

FOURTH SUNDAY OF ORDINARY TIME (40c)

READING:

Jeremiah 1:4-5, 17-19 Before your birth I knew you. I appoint you prophet to the nations.

Psalm 71 I will sing of your salvation.

1 Corinthians 12:31–13:13 "If I have not love I am nothing. . . . Three things will last . . . and the greatest is love."

Luke 4:21-30 Facing the unbelief of the people at Nazareth, Jesus recalls that prophets are without honor in their native place.

CATECHISM:

+ **871-873** Mission of the laity. Equality and difference in the Church.
+ **436** Role of the prophet.
+ **904-907** Participation in Christ's prophetic office.
+ **1822-1829** The virtue of charity.
+ **2258-2262, 2270-2275** Life: sacred from the womb (Fifth Commandment).
+ **2465-2474** Truth: essential to human relationships. The Christian mission as witnesses to the truth.

FIFTH SUNDAY OF
ORDINARY TIME (5Oc)

READING:

Isaiah 6:1-2, 3-8 Isaiah, a man of unclean lips, beholds the Lord's glory in the temple and is sent on mission.

Psalm 138 In the sight of the angels I will sing your praises, Lord.

1 Corinthians 15:1-11 St. Paul speaks of his call to preach nothing but Christ crucified and risen from the dead.

Luke 5:1-11 Simon, aware of his own sinfulness, responds to the mission of Jesus by becoming a disciple.

CATECHISM:

+ **208** God's mysterious presence (cites first reading and Gospel).
+ **425** Vocation of disciple to preach Christ.
+ **1816** Disciple gives witness to faith.
+ **858-860** The apostles' mission.
+ **863-865** Apostolate of the Church.
+ **1548-1553** Ordained ministry: represents Christ, serves community, not freed from human limitations.

SIXTH SUNDAY OF
ORDINARY TIME (6Oc)

READING:

Jeremiah 17:5-8 Cursed is the one who trusts in human beings. Blessed is the one who trusts in the Lord like a tree beside the waters.

Psalm 1 Blessed are they who hope in the Lord.

1 Corinthians 15:12, 16-20 If the dead are not raised, then Christ has not been raised, and your faith is in vain.

Luke 6:17, 20-26 The beatitudes and the woes.

CATECHISM:

+ **310, 2086** The Lord upholds creation.
+ **2443-2449** Love of the poor.
+ **1965-1974** The New Law.
+ **2544-2550** Poverty of heart.
+ **989-991, 1002-1003** Hope in the Resurrection.
+ **1716-1724** Desire for happiness. The beatitudes.
+ **632-635** Christ's descent into hell. Solidarity with all the dead.

SEVENTH SUNDAY OF ORDINARY TIME (7Oc)

READING:

1 Samuel 26:2, 7-9, 12-13, 22-23 Saul was delivered into the hands of David, his enemy, although no harm came to him as he was recognized as the Lord's anointed.

Psalm 103 The Lord is kind and merciful.

1 Corinthians 15:45-49 We are called to mirror and image the mercy and forgiveness the Lord has won for us.

Luke 6:27-38 Be merciful as your Father is merciful.

CATECHISM:

> + **356-361** Human beings as "image of God," perfectly revealed in Christ, the New Adam.
> + **1886-1889** Conversion and society.
> + **504** Christ as New Adam.
> + **460** Christ became flesh so that we could share the divine nature.
> + **1789** The Golden Rule.

EIGHTH SUNDAY OF ORDINARY TIME (8Oc)

READING:

Sirach 27:4-7 One's words will reveal one's inner self.

Psalm 92 Lord, it is good to give thanks to you.

1 Corinthians 15:54-58 "Death, where is your victory?" We have victory through Christ Jesus.

Luke 6:39-45 "Remove the beam from your own eye first." A person speaks from what is in the heart.

CATECHISM:

> ✝ **1749-1756** Good and evil acts. Sources of morality.
> ✝ **1987-1988, 1993-1995** Grace of the Holy Spirit and justification.
> ✝ **2464-2470, 2475-2487** Living in and preserving the truth (Eighth Commandment).
> ✝ **2515-2519** Flesh and spirit. The heart as seat of moral personality (Sixth Commandment).

NINTH SUNDAY OF ORDINARY TIME (9Oc)

READING:

1 Kings 8:41-43 Solomon's prayer that the temple be a home for all people.

Psalm 117 Go out to all the world and tell the Good News.

Galatians 1:1-2, 6-10 Paul seeks fidelity to Christ rather than human beings.

Luke 7:1-10 The centurion asks Jesus to heal his slave: "I am not worthy to have you enter under my roof . . . but say the word." Jesus remarks, "Not even in Israel have I found such faith."

CATECHISM:

+ **425-429** Christ: the heart of preaching and catechesis.
+ **1503-1505** Christ the Physician. Faith in the signs of the kingdom.
+ **543, 547-548** Everyone is called to the kingdom (manifested in signs).
+ **775-776** Church: sacrament of universal salvation.
+ **1385-1386** Coming to the Eucharist with humble faith.
+ **142-144, 151** Obedient faith. Response of faith to God's revelation. Faith in Jesus.
+ **2580** Solomon's prayer in the temple.

TENTH SUNDAY OF
ORDINARY TIME (10Oc)

READING:

1 Kings 17:17-24 Elijah heals the son of the widow of Zarephath.

Psalm 30 I will praise you, Lord, for you have rescued me.

Galatians 1:1-19 Paul receives direct call by God to know Christ and proclaim his Gospel.

Luke 7:11-17 Jesus raises the son of the widow of Nain.

CATECHISM:

✝ **2583** Elijah learns mercy and teaches the widow to believe in God's Word.

✝ **442, 659** Paul came to faith in the Son of God.

✝ **992-994** Raising the dead to life. Sign of Christ's own Resurrection.

✝ **1683-1690, 2299-2301** The Church's ministry at the time of death. Respect for the dead.

ELEVENTH SUNDAY OF ORDINARY TIME (11Oc)

READING:

2 Samuel 12:7-10, 13 God forgives David's sin, but trouble will remain in David's house.

Psalm 32 Lord, you forgave the wrong I have done.

Galatians 2:16, 19-21 Justification by faith rather than by the works of the Law. "I live no longer I but Christ lives in me."

Luke 7:36–8:3 Jesus at the Pharisee's dinner. The sinful woman washes and anoints his feet. "Much is forgiven her who has shown great love."

CATECHISM:

+ **1731-1736** Freedom and moral responsibility.
+ **574-576, 588-589** Jesus scandalizes some of Israel's leaders.
+ **1441, 1450-1454** Only God forgives sins. The sinner's sorrow.
+ **1459, 1472-1473** The punishments because of sin. Forgiveness and satisfaction.
+ **1965-1968, 1972** The Law of the Gospel. Acting out of God's love infused into us.
+ **2517-2522** Purification of the heart. Battle for purity (Ninth Commandment).

TWELFTH SUNDAY OF ORDINARY TIME (12Oc)

READING:

Zechariah 12:10-11 With lament "they shall look on him whom they have pierced." But God will open for the people a purifying fountain.

Psalm 63 My soul is thirsting for you, O Lord my God.

Galatians 3:26-29 Through baptism all are one in Christ. No Jew or Greek, male or female.

Luke 9:18-24 "Who do they say that I am?" Peter's profession of faith and Christ's prediction of the Passion.

CATECHISM:

✝ **790-791** Baptismal grace overcomes division.
✝ **1430-1432** Call to conversion of the human heart: recognition of our sin and the greatness of God's love.
✝ **2599-2600** Jesus: example of prayer.
✝ **436, 440-442, 606-607, 618, 1440** Jesus: the "Christ," the "Son of God" who must suffer. Our following the way of the cross.

THIRTEENTH SUNDAY OF ORDINARY TIME (13Oc)

READING:

1 Kings 19:16, 19-21 Elisha is appointed prophet to succeed Elijah.

Psalm 16 You are my inheritance, O Lord.

Galatians 5:1, 13-18 Called to freedom. Serve one another in love, guided by the Spirit rather than the flesh.

Luke 9:51-62 Journey to Jerusalem. Jesus, who has nowhere to lay his head, seeks resolute followers.

CATECHISM:

+ **1739-1742** Freedom, sin, and grace.
+ **2488-2492** Prudent discretion in speaking the truth about others.
+ **362-364, 1762-1770, 2515-2516** Body and soul. Passions and the moral life. Rebellion of flesh against the spirit.
+ **2338-2345** Self-mastery and chastity (Sixth Commandment).
+ **2541-2543** Desires of the Spirit: turning from avarice and envy.
+ **544, 557** Jesus identifies with the lowly and dispossessed. He journeys to suffer in Jerusalem.

FOURTEENTH SUNDAY OF ORDINARY TIME (14Oc)

READING:

Isaiah 66:10-14 Rejoice with Jerusalem. God spreads prosperity like a river. God comforts as a mother does her child.

Psalm 66 Let all the earth cry out to God with joy.

Galatians 6:14-18 Boasting only in the cross of Christ, who brings about a new creation.

Luke 10:1-12, 17-20 The disciples are sent out. The harvest is abundant. "The kingdom of God is at hand." Satan falls like lightning from the sky.

CATECHISM:

+ **628, 1214** Baptism into newness of life.
+ **542, 765, 787, 851** Gathering all into the family of God. The disciples share Christ's mission and fate.
+ **1235, 2015** The mark of the cross on the Christian. Path to holiness.
+ **2611** Disciples should pray that they may cooperate with the divine plan.
+ **2429-2436** Justice in employment and wages.
+ **539, 2851-2852** Christ conquers Satan. "Deliver us from evil."

FIFTEENTH SUNDAY OF ORDINARY TIME (15Oc)

READING:

Deuteronomy 30:10-14 Return to Lord with whole heart and soul. His command is not far from you.

Psalm 69 Turn to the Lord in your need and you will live. **Or Psalm 19** Your words, Lord, are Spirit and life.

Colossians 1:15-20 Christ: image of the invisible God, through whom all things were made.

Luke 10:25-37 "What must I do to inherit eternal life?" Love God with whole heart and your neighbor. The compassionate Samaritan.

CATECHISM:

+ **792** Christ: preeminent. Head of the Body.
+ **299, 1701-1702** Born of the Word: The goodness of the world and the dignity of human persons.
+ **294, 2641** Church moved to praise God for the goodness of the divine plan established in Christ.
+ **2052-2055, 2083** Love God. Love your neighbor.
+ **1825, 1931-1933, 2447** All-embracing charity. Look upon one's neighbor as another self.
+ **1159-1162** Christ-centered use of holy images.

SIXTEENTH SUNDAY OF
ORDINARY TIME (16Oc)

READING:

Genesis 18:1-10 Abraham welcomes three strangers who foretell that Sarah will bear a son.

Psalm 15 He who does justice will live in the presence of the Lord.

Colossians 1:24-28 In my flesh I fill up what is lacking in the afflictions of Christ. God's hidden mystery is revealed among his holy ones.

Luke 10:38-42 Martha welcomes Jesus. Mary chooses the better part.

CATECHISM:

+ **2558-2571** Prayer as gift, covenant, communion. Universal call to prayer.
+ **705-706** Spirit of the promise to humanity first entrusted to Abraham and culminating in Christ.
+ **307, 618, 1508** Human beings enter deliberately into God's plan by actions and sufferings.
+ **51-53, 142-144, 436** God meets human beings as friends, reveals his loving plan, and invites them into his company. Communion with Christ: the purpose of catechesis.

SEVENTEENTH SUNDAY OF ORDINARY TIME (17Oc)

READING:

Genesis 18:20-32 Abraham intercedes with God to save Sodom and Gomorrah.

Psalm 138 Lord, on the day I called for help, you answered me.

Colossians 2:12-14 Buried with him in baptism, raised with him in faith.

Luke 11:1-13 The Lord's Prayer.

CATECHISM:

+ **2759-2766** Our Father.
+ **728** "To his disciples he speaks openly of the Spirit in connection with prayer."
+ **2571** Abraham, being attuned to God, dares to intercede.
+ **2601, 2609-2614** By contemplating and hearing the Son, the master of prayer, the children learn to pray — with faith, boldness and persistence.
+ **2777-2785, 2803-2806** The Father, the seven petitions of the Lord's Prayer.
+ **2738** Christian prayer is in cooperation with God's providence, his plan of love for men.
+ **2697-2699** The Life of Prayer.
+ **1002-1004** Risen with Christ.

EIGHTEENTH SUNDAY OF ORDINARY TIME (18Oc)

READING:

Ecclesiastes 1:2, 2:21-23 "All things are vanity." "What profit comes to a man from all the toil and anxiety of heart with which he has labored under the sun?"

Psalm 90 If today you hear his voice, harden not your hearts.

Colossians 3:1-5, 9-11 Mystical death and Resurrection. Renunciation of vice.

Luke 12:13-21 Saying against greed. Parable of the rich fool. Stored up so many things: eat, drink! True wealth: rich in the sight of God.

CATECHISM:

+ **2598-2616** Christ: Model and Teacher of Prayer.
+ **628** New life in Christ.
+ **655** "Their lives are swept up by Christ into the heart of divine life."
+ **1002-1004** Risen with Christ.
+ **1227** We have "put on Christ." Baptism purifies, justifies and sanctifies.
+ **1694** Christians are dead to sin and alive in God. Conform thoughts, words and actions to mind of Christ.
+ **2534-2543** The wayward heart covets what belongs to another (Tenth Commandment).

NINETEENTH SUNDAY OF ORDINARY TIME (19Oc)

READING:

Wisdom 18:6-9 In the secret obedience of Passover, God's people awaited salvation.

Psalm 33 Blessed the people the Lord has chosen to be his own.

Hebrews 11:1-2, 8-19 (or 11:1-2, 8-12) Faith: evidence of things not seen. By faith Abraham obeyed and sojourned. He did not receive what had been promised, but saw it from afar.

Luke 12:32-48 (or 12:35-40) Be vigilant for the master's return. He will serve them at table.

CATECHISM:

+ **2623-2625** Major kinds of prayer.
+ **716** The Holy Spirit works in the poor who humbly await God's justice.
+ **145-147, 2570-2573** Abraham, the father of all who believe, is conformed to the likeness of God.
+ **2728-2734, 2849** Prayer as humble vigilance and filial trust despite setback and struggle.
+ **1817-1819** Virtue of hope. Abraham's example.

TWENTIETH SUNDAY OF ORDINARY TIME (20Oc)

READING:

Jeremiah 38:4-6, 8-10 God's servant thrown into the cistern, then saved.

Psalm 40 Lord, come to my aid!

Hebrews 12:1-4 With the "cloud of witnesses," persevere. Keep eyes on Jesus, our leader and perfecter of faith.

Luke 12:49-53 Jesus: a cause of division. "There is a baptism with which I must be baptized, and how great my anguish is until it is accomplished!"

CATECHISM:

+ **165** Witnesses of faith. Cloud of witnesses. "Look to Jesus the pioneer and perfecter of our faith."
+ **536-537, 606-609, 1225** "Baptism": Jesus yearns to embrace the Father's plan of love.
+ **575-576** Jesus: sign of contradiction.
+ **2738-2745, 2803-2804** Prayer: trusting in God. Persevering in love. The burning desire for God's will to be done.

TWENTY-FIRST SUNDAY OF ORDINARY TIME (21Oc)

READING:

Isaiah 66:18-21 Gathering of the nations to Jerusalem.

Psalm 117 Go out to all the world and tell the Good News.

Hebrews 12:5-7, 11-13 Do not disdain the discipline of the Lord.

Luke 13:22-30 The narrow gate. Wailing when you are cast out and the nations are welcomed to the kingdom's table.

CATECHISM:

+ **543-545** All are called to the kingdom. Even sinners are invited to the table, but only humble hearts can enter.
+ **360-361, 775-776** Essential unity of human race. Church: sacrament of salvation for all.
+ **1033-1037, 1427-1429** Exclusion from salvation. The urgent call to conversion. Conversion as the continuing task of the whole Church.
+ **142-144, 2825-2827** Faith: obedient submission to God even as Jesus practiced it.

TWENTY-SECOND SUNDAY OF ORDINARY TIME (22Oc)

READING:

Sirach 3:17-18, 20, 28-29 Humility of God's child.

Psalm 68 God, in your goodness, you have made a home for the poor.

Hebrews 12:18-19, 22-24 You have approached Mount Zion. The festal gathering. Assembly of the firstborn. Jesus, mediator of a New Covenant.

Luke 14:1, 7-14 Conduct of guests at dinner. "My friend, move up." Invite the poor and lame. You will be repaid in the Resurrection.

CATECHISM:

+ **1730-1742** Grandeur of true human freedom. False visions of freedom.
+ **758-762, 1136-1141** Church: God's plan to gather up all people in loving communion. Begun at creation, deepened in Old Covenant, fulfilled in New Covenant, and celebrated in liturgy.
+ **543-546** The kingdom belongs to the humble of heart.
+ **588-589** Jesus challenges customary patterns. Salvation for the poor, the sinner.
+ **2544-2547** Call to poverty of heart.

TWENTY-THIRD SUNDAY OF ORDINARY TIME (23Oc)

READING:

Wisdom 9:13-18 We can scarcely guess earthly things. Who can know God's counsel — except that God gives wisdom.

Psalm 90 In every age, O Lord, you have been our refuge.

Philemon 9-10, 12-17 Welcome Onesimus not as slave but as brother.

Luke 14:25-33 To be worthy of Christ: renounce family, possessions, and life. Carry the cross. Consider the cost.

CATECHISM:

+ **36-43** How can we know or speak about God?
+ **2414** Enslavement of human beings (Seventh Commandment).
+ **1618** The bond with Christ takes precedence over all other bonds, familial or social.
+ **2544-2547** Poverty of heart. "Jesus enjoins his disciples to prefer him to everything and every one."
+ **914-919, 925-927** The consecrated life. Seeking first the kingdom.

TWENTY-FOURTH SUNDAY OF ORDINARY TIME (24Oc)

READING:

Exodus 32:7-11, 13-14 Idolatry of the stiff-necked people. The Lord relents in punishment.

Psalm 51 I will rise and go to my Father.

1 Timothy 1:12-17 Paul the sinner, and his gratitude for God's mercy.

Luke 15:1-32 (or 15:1-10) Parables: lost sheep, coin, and son.

CATECHISM:

+ **2084-2086, 2110-2132** "Have no other gods." Idolatry, magic, irreligion (First Commandment).
+ **2574-2577** Moses and the prayer of the mediator.
+ **1432, 1439** A new heart. The prodigal son as example of conversion.
+ **210-211, 604-605** In the face of sin, God acts with mercy and concern.

TWENTY-FIFTH SUNDAY OF ORDINARY TIME (25Oc)

READING:

Amos 8:4-7 Do not exploit the weak. Avoid greed.

Psalm 113 Praise the Lord who lifts up the poor.

1 Timothy 2:1-8 Let prayers be offered for every one. God wills that all be saved. One God, one Mediator.

Luke 16:1-13 Parable of the dishonest steward.

CATECHISM:

2407-2409, 2414, 2535-2537 Temperance and justice. Preserving the rights of others. Greed (Seventh and Tenth Commandments).

2422-2425, 2443-2446 Economic justice. Love for the poor (Seventh Commandment).

2634-2636, 851 Prayer of intercession; Christian community prays for all, urged on by God's love.

2700-2704 Tradition of vocal prayer.

2842-2845 "As we forgive those who trespass against us."

TWENTY-SIXTH SUNDAY OF ORDINARY TIME (26Oc)

READING:

Amos 6:1, 4-7 The satiated and complacent shall be the first to go into exile.

Psalm 146 Praise the Lord, my soul!

1 Timothy 6:11-16 Pursue righteousness, devotion, faith, love, patience, and gentleness until the appearance of the Lord.

Luke 16:19-31 Parable of the rich man and Lazarus.

CATECHISM:

> ✝ **2831** Hunger, solidarity, and the prayer, "Give us this day our daily bread."
>
> ✝ **2437-2442** Justice and solidarity among the nations.
>
> ✝ **2443-2449** Love for the poor.
>
> ✝ **1934-1940** Equality and differences among people. Solidarity.
>
> ✝ **633, 1021-1022** The "abode of the dead." The particular judgment.
>
> ✝ **334-336** Care of the angels.

TWENTY-SEVENTH SUNDAY OF ORDINARY TIME (27Oc)

READING:

Habakkuk 1:2-3, 2:2-4 Violence, ruin, strife! But the vision has its time. The just one, because of his faith, shall live.

Psalm 95 If today you hear his voice, harden not your hearts.

2 Timothy 1:6-8, 13-14 Stir into flame the gift of God that you had through the imposition of my hands.

Luke 17:5-10 Faith like a mustard seed. "We are servants who have done merely what was expected."

CATECHISM:

+ **84-87** The "rich trust" of faith. Magisterium.
+ **162** Hold on to and grow in faith.
+ **876** Ecclesial minister. Role as servant.
+ **711-716, 1820** God's people humbly await the Messiah. Hope under trial.
+ **798-801** The Holy Spirit graces us with gifts for the common good.

TWENTY-EIGHTH SUNDAY OF ORDINARY TIME (28Oc)

READING:

2 Kings 5:1-17 Healing of Naaman.

Psalm 98 The Lord has revealed to the nations his saving power.

2 Timothy 2:8-13 No chaining the Word of God. If we have died with him, we shall also live with him.

Luke 17:11-19 Ten lepers. One — a Samaritan — returns in thanks. "Your faith has saved you."

CATECHISM:

+ **2629-2633, 2637-2638** Prayer of petition. Prayer of thanksgiving.
+ **101-108** The living Word of God. In Christ, in human words.
+ **537, 628, 655, 1005-1011, 1214** Dying and rising in Christ through baptism and through our earthly end.
+ **547-549, 1503** Jesus' healings as signs of the kingdom.
+ **2288-2291** Care for physical health (Fifth Commandment).

TWENTY-NINTH SUNDAY OF ORDINARY TIME (29Oc)

READING:

Exodus 17:8-13 With help, Moses keeps his hands raised up, and Israel conquers.

Psalm 121 Our help is from the Lord, who made heaven and earth.

2 Timothy 3:14–4:2 Remain faithful. Sacred Scriptures are inspired, capable of giving wisdom.

Luke 18:1-8 Persistent widow.

CATECHISM:

+ **109-114, 131-133** Scripture: interpretation and place in Church's life.
+ **2574-2577, 2634-2636** Moses the mediator. Prayers of intercession.
+ **2573, 2725-2728, 2742-2745** Pray constantly, despite its struggle.
+ **2307-2317** Morality of war (Fifth Commandment).

THIRTIETH SUNDAY OF ORDINARY TIME (30Oc)

READING:

Sirach 35:15-17, 20-22 Prayer of the lowly pierces the clouds. He who serves God willingly is heard.

Psalm 34 The Lord hears the cry of the poor.

2 Timothy 4:6-8, 16-18 The Lord gave me strength.

Luke 18:9-14 Prayer of the pharisee and the tax collector.

CATECHISM:

+ **2015-2016** Christian holiness and the cross. The grace of final perseverance.
+ **588, 2559-2561, 2616, 2626-2628, 2631** Sinners before God. Prayer: God's gift arising in humble hearts. Adoration.
+ **2588-2589** Psalms: cry of the heart. Simplicity and spontaneity of prayer.

THIRTY-FIRST SUNDAY
OF ORDINARY TIME (31Oc)

READING:

Wisdom 11:22–12:1 "You love all you have made, sparing them because they are yours, with the imperishable spirit in all things."

Psalm 145 I will praise your name forever, my king and my God.

2 Thessalonians 1:11–2:2 May God make you worthy of his calling. Do not be shaken by rumors that the day of the Lord is at hand.

Luke 19:1-10 Zacchaeus received Jesus with joy. "The Son of Man comes to save what was lost."

CATECHISM:

+ **295-301** Out of nothing God creates a good world with wisdom and love. He is present to it and sustains it.
+ **588-589, 1443** Jesus welcomes sinners and through forgiveness restores them to God's community — signified by table sharing.
+ **2639, 2709-2719** Prayer of praise. Contemplative prayer.
+ **60** Descendants of Abraham. Trustees of the promise that is fulfilled when God gathers all his children into the Church's unity.
+ **2411-2412** Reparation for injustice (Seventh Commandment).

THIRTY-SECOND SUNDAY OF ORDINARY TIME (32Oc)

READING:

2 Maccabees 7:1-2, 9-14 Seven brothers and mother. Submit to death at human hands trusting that the King of the world will raise them to live forever.

Psalm 17 Lord, when your glory appears, my joy will be full.

2 Thessalonians 2:16–3:5 The Lord is faithful. May the Lord encourage your hearts in good deeds.

Luke 20:27-38 (or 20:27, 34-38) Discussion with the Sadducees about the Resurrection. "Not God of the dead, but of the living."

CATECHISM:

+ **958-959** Communion of life and prayer with the dead.
+ **992-1001** Progressive revelation of the Resurrection: who, how, when.
+ **2104-2106** Duty to honor God. Freedom from religious coercion.
+ **2848-2849** Prayer for a strong and vigilant heart in face of trial. "Lead us not into temptation."
+ **1023-1029** Heaven: destiny of those who die in God's grace.
+ **1030-1032** Final purification of those who die in God's friendship but are still imperfect (purgatory).

THIRTY-THIRD SUNDAY OF ORDINARY TIME (33Oc)

READING:

Malachi 3:19-20 The blazing day of the Lord. Reducing the evil to stubble but like the healing sun for those who fear God's name.

Psalm 98 The Lord comes to rule the earth with justice.

2 Thessalonians 3:7-12 Imitate our hard work. Anyone unwilling to work should not eat.

Luke 21:5-19 The destruction of the temple foretold and coming persecution. "By perseverance you will secure your lives."

CATECHISM:

+ **2426-2429** Human work: duty, vocation.
+ **2828-2837** "Give us this day our daily bread."
+ **675-679** The Church's ultimate trial.
+ **583-586** Jesus and the temple.
+ **162-165** Persevering in faith. The beginning of eternal life.

CHRIST THE KING

READING:

2 Samuel 5:1-3 The tribes recognize and anoint David as king.

Psalm 122 Let us go rejoicing to the house of the Lord.

Colossians 1:12-20 Christ: the image of the invisible God. The first-born of all creation.

Luke 23:35-43 They jeered, "If you are King of the Jews, save yourself." "Remember me when you come into your kingdom." "Today you will be with me in Paradise."

CATECHISM:

+ **436-440** Christ's divine mission. Sent to inaugurate kingdom.
+ **450** Christ's leadership over world.
+ **624** Christ tastes death to bring peace to whole world.
+ **668-670** Christ already reigns through the Church.
+ **241** "Image of the invisible God" as the "radiance of the glory of God" and "the very stamp of his nature."
+ **2579-2580** David as image of the good king who shepherds and prays for his people.

TRANSFIGURATION OF THE LORD (AUGUST 6)

READING:

Daniel 7:9-10; 13-14 Ancient one. Myriads attended. Son of Man given rule.

Psalm 97 The Lord is king, the most high over all the earth.

2 Peter 1:16-19 Not myths: We ourselves heard and saw his splendor.

Luke 9:28b-36 Transfigured in glory, the Son of Man has received kingship and dominion.

CATECHISM:

+ **554-556** Transfiguration — a foretaste of the kingdom.
+ **422-424, 606-608** The whole life of the Beloved Son among us is an offering to the Father.
+ **660-664** The glory and dominion of the Risen One at the Father's right hand.
+ **2794-2796** The majesty of the Father who is "in heaven."
+ **2583** Moses and Elijah: finding God in varied ways, now they see the unveiled face of Christ.

ASSUMPTION OF THE BLESSED VIRGIN

READING:

Revelation 11:19; 12:1-6; 10 Great sign. Woman clothed with the sun. Her newborn child is saved from the devouring dragon.

Psalm 45 The queen stands at your right hand, arrayed in gold.

1 Corinthians 15:20-26 In Adam all die. In Christ all will come to life as he conquers every enemy, even death itself.

Luke 1:39-56 Visit to Elizabeth: "Blessed is she who believed." Magnificat.

CATECHISM:

+ **1138** Celebrants of the heavenly liturgy.
+ **410-412, 495, 655, 1008** Adam's death and Mary, the New Eve. Christ's Resurrection and the destiny of his Church.
+ **668, 671-672** Christ reigns until all things are subjected to him. The distress of the Church as it waits.
+ **717, 721-726** The Holy Spirit works in Mary, the New Eve.
+ **273, 2617-2619** The prayer of the Virgin Mary.
+ **964-970** Mary: united with Christ — also in her Assumption — is our Mother in the order of grace.

SOLEMNITY OF ALL SAINTS

READING:

Revelation 7:2-4, 9-14 A crowd that no one could number. They washed their robes in blood of Lamb.

Psalm 24 Lord, this is the people that longs to see your face.

1 John 3:1-3 The Father's love: we are God's children now. Then we will be like him.

Matthew 5:1-12 On the mountain, Jesus teaches the beatitudes.

CATECHISM:

+ **1138, 2642** The heavenly liturgy. Its celebrants. Its prayer of praise.
+ **1296** The "seal" of God's servants (confirmation).
+ **163-164** Faith: tasting in advance the beatific vision, even amid trials.
+ **1023-1024** Heaven: seeing God face-to-face. Communion of life and love with the Most Holy Trinity.
+ **1161** Mary and the saints: participants in world's salvation and in communion with us (holy images).
+ **1716-1724** Our vocation to beatitude.
+ **520** Christ, our model of holiness.
+ **828-829, 946-948, 954-957, 1173** The Church is holy. The communion of saints. Memorials of the saints.
+ **1474-1477** Sharing the treasury of the communion of saints relating to indulgences.
+ **2683-2684** The saints as examples of prayer.

+ Index of Themes

The major catechetical themes are listed according to the **bold-faced** numbered sections from the *Catechism of the Catholic Church*. After each numbered section is a statement of the basic theme of that section. This is followed by the list of the Sundays or feasts associated with those themes from the Scripture readings for the three-year Lectionary cycle. The Sundays are identified by number, season, and cycle according to the following legend:

Legend (examples):

5La	Fifth Sunday of Lent, Cycle A
6Eb	Sixth Sunday of Easter, Cycle B
11Oa	Eleventh Sunday of Ordinary Time, Cycle A
2Aa	Second Sunday of Advent, Cycle A

1-25 Coming to know and love God. Professing and handing on faith.

5Lc, 6Eb, 7Ea, Trinity b, 9Oc, 11Oa

25, 864, 1889, 2055 All of Christian life and teaching must be directed to love.

6Eb, 13Ob, 23Oa, 30Oa

27-30 Desire for God in the human heart.

Epiphany a

31-38 The desire for God. Our hearts yearn for God ceaselessly.

Epiphany c, 23Oc

39-43 Speaking about God. The limits of our language.

Epiphany c

50-53 God reveals himself and his divine plan inviting us to communion with himself.

2Aa, 4Aa, Christmas c, Baptism of Lord c, 16Oc, 25Oa

54-67 Stages of revelation and its completion in Jesus.

1Aa, 2Aa, 3Aa, Christmas a, b, c, Baptism of Lord c, 2Lc, Easter Vigil, 2Oa, 31Oc

74-83 God's Word as given to us through Sacred Scripture and tradition.

4Ec, 6Ec, 22Ob, 29Oa

84-95 The Magisterium serves the faith by guarding the deposit of faith and helping the faithful to grasp it rightly.

Pentecost b, Trinity c, 22Ob, 27Oc

101-108 Sacred Scripture is the inspired Word of God.

4Aa, b, c, 2Lb, 15Oa, 28Ob, 28Oc

109-133 The senses of Scripture and the canon (Old and New Testament).

Epiphany c, 2Lb, 3Ea, 3Oc, 28Ob, 29Oc, 31Oa

142-152 Faith: the meaning and the gladness of faith. The obedience of faith.

4Aa, b, c, Baptism of Lord c, Easter Vigil, 6Eb, Pentecost a, 9Oc, 10Oa, 16Oc, 19Oa, 19Oc, 21Oc

153-165 Characteristics of faith, particularly seeing faith as a "gift" from God.

3La, 3Lb, 2Ec, 4Eb, Ascension b, 5Oa, 11Ob, 12Ob, 14Oa, 19Oa, 20Oa, 20Oc, 21Oa, 27Oc, 33Oc, Christ the King b, All Saints

166-175 Faith as both a personal and ecclesial act.

2Ec, 11Ob

185-197 The Profession of Faith: The creed as the continuous profession of the one faith handed down from the apostles.

Easter c, 4Ea, Trinity b

199-213 "I believe in God, the Father almighty": God as Creator of all things.

3Lc, 2Eb, Trinity a, 5Oc, 22Ob, 24Oc, 25Oa, 31Ob

215-227 God is truth and God is love. The difference that believing in God makes.

4Lb, 6Eb, 7Eb, Trinity c, 6Oa, 8Ob, 30Oa, 31Ob

232-248 God as Father: God is the first origin of everything and at the same time goodness and love.

6Ec, Pentecost b, Trinity a, b, c, 14Oa, 31Oa, Christ the King c

249-256 The mystery of Most Holy Trinity is the central mystery of faith.

2La, 3Lb, Trinity a

257-260 Saving acts of the Trinity. God dwelling in us.

3Lb, Easter Vigil, 6Ec, 7Ec, Trinity b, 15Ob, 17Oa, Christ the King a, 19Ob

268-274 God is almighty. Nothing is impossible with God.

4Aa, 3Lb, Easter Vigil, Easter c, 4Oa, 14Ob, 28Oa, Assumption

279-301 God is Creator of all things. The wonder of God's creating everything out of nothing, of creation, and of God's keeping all things in being.

1Ab, Easter Vigil, 6Oc, 8Oa, 11Ob, 12Ob, 15Oa, 15Oc, 16Ob, 18Oa, 31Oc, Christ the King a

302-308 God carries out his plan. Divine providence.

4Ea, 8Oa, 12Oa, 12Ob, 16Ob, 16Oc, 29Oa

309-314 Human freedom and the problem of evil.

4Lb, 6Oc, 12Ob, 16Oa, 17Oa

328-336 The existence and meaning of angels.

17Oa, 26Oc

337-349 God's creation of the material world and its inherent goodness.

9Ob, 10Ob

355-361 Greatness of the human person. God created man and woman in his own image and likeness.

Epiphany c, Easter Vigil, 7Oc, 13Ob, 16Ob, 21Oc, 30Oa

362-368 The human person is made up of a unity of the body and soul.

1La, 2Ob, 12Oa, 13Ob, 13Oc, 22Oa, 30Oa

369-373 Male and female, he created them. Unity and differentiation. Meaning of human sexuality as God intended.

27Ob

374-379 The state of original holiness and the existence of paradise. Man in Paradise.

Immaculate Conception a, Immaculate Conception b, 1La, 10Ob

385-390 The fall and the serious reality of original sin.

1Ab, Immaculate Conception b, 10Ob, 16Oa

391-395 The fall of the angels. The personal reality of Satan.

9Oa, 10Ob, 13Ob, 18Oa

396-409 The consequences of original sin.

Immaculate Conception a, Immaculate Conception b, 1La, 5La, Easter Vigil, 2Oa, 4Oa, 9Oa, 10Ob, 12Oa, 15Oa

410-412 God's faithfulness after mankind sinned.

1La, Easter Vigil, 10Ob, Assumption

422-429 The Good News of Jesus is at the heart of our faith. The transmission of the Christian faith is primarily the proclamation of Jesus Christ.

Christmas a, Christmas c, Mother of God a, 5Lc, 7Ec, 5Oc, 9Oc, 21Oa, Transfiguration

430-440 Jesus means "God saves." Christ means "the Anointed One." Jesus is the Light of the World.

4Aa, Epiphany a, Baptism of Lord c, 1Lc, 5Lb, Holy Thursday, Ascension b, 4Eb, 6Eb, 3Oc, 4Ob, 4Oc, 9Oa, 12Oc, 16Oc, 20Oa, 21Oa, 24Ob, 29Ob, 31Oa, Christ the King c

441-451 Jesus is the only Son of God. Difference between "true and only" son and adoptive sons and daughters. He is what the Father is.

Baptism of Lord a, Passion a, b, c, 1Lc, 10Oc, 12Oc, 19Oa, 21Oa, 29Oa, Christ the King c

456-463 The Son of God became man. The mystery of the Incarnation.

Christmas a, b, c, 4Lb, Easter Vigil, 4Eb, 7Oc, 14Oa, 26Oa

464-469 Jesus, who is our God, truly became also our Brother. He is True God and True Man. The second person of the Trinity.

4Ab, Christmas a, b, Mother of God a, Trinity c

471-474 Christ's soul and his human knowledge.

24Ob

478 The Sacred Heart of the Incarnate Word.

Christmas a, c, 2Eb

484-489 Jesus was conceived by the Holy Spirit and born of the Virgin Mary.

4Aa, Mother of God b, 2Oa

490-494 Mary's Immaculate Conception: its meaning and importance.

4Ab, Immaculate Conception a, b, c

495 Mary is truly the mother of God. Theotokos.

4Ac, Mother of God a, b, c, Assumption

496-507 The Virginity of Mary and its importance to us.

4Aa, 4Ac, Mother of God b, 7Oc

512-521 The importance and characteristics of the blessed mysteries of Christ's life.

Holy Family a, Epiphany c, Holy Thursday, 3Eb, 5Ea, Ascension c, 4Oa, 12Ob, 31Oa, All Saints

522-533 The mysteries of Christ's infancy and hidden life.

2Aa, Christmas a, b, c, Holy Family a, b, c, Mother of God a, Epiphany a, b, c, 2Oa, 2Ob, 27Oa

534 The finding of Jesus in the temple.

Holy Family c

535-537 The meaning of the baptism of Jesus.

2Aa, Baptism of Lord a, b, c, 13Oa, 20Oc, 26Oa, 28Oc, 29Ob

538-540 The temptations of Christ.

1La, b, c, 14Oc

541-553 Jesus and the proclamation of the Kingdom of God.

3Aa, 4Lc, 3Ec, 3Ob, 3Oc, 4Oa, 4Ob, 5Ob, 9Oc, 10Oa, 10Ob, 11Oa, 12Ob, 13Oc, 14Oa, 14Oc, 15Oa, 17Ob, 20Oa, 20Ob, 21Oa, 21Oc, 22Oc, 23Oa, 25Oa, 26Oa, 28Oa, 28Oc, 30Ob, Christ the King a

554-556 The Transfiguration of Jesus.

2La, 2Lc, 22Oa, Transfiguration

557-560 Going up to Jerusalem: Jesus' longing to save us.

2Lc, Passion (Palm Gospel) a, b, c, 13Oc, 14Oa, 31Oa

571-572 Christ's Paschal mystery is the heart of the Good News. "He suffered under Pontius Pilate."

Passion a, Passion b, 24Ob

574-591 Jesus as the "sign of contradiction."

3La, 3Lb, 4Lc, 6Oa, 10Oa, 11Oc, 20Oc, 22Ob, 22Oc, 25Oa, 26Oa, 30Oc, 31Oa, 31Oc, 33Oc

595-598 All sinners were authors of Christ's Passion.

Passion b, c, Good Friday, 3Eb, 4Ec

599-605 Christ's redeeming death in God's saving plan.

4Lb, 4Lc, 5Lb, Good Friday, Easter Vigil, Easter a, b, c, 2Ea, 3Eb, 4Eb, 4Ec, 7Eb, 11Oa, 12Oa, 15Ob, 24Ob, 24Oc, 25Ob, 26Oa, 29Ob

606-612 Jesus freely offered himself for the salvation of sinners.

4Lb, 5Lb, Passion a, Passion c, Holy Thursday, 4Eb, 4Ec, 6Eb, 7Eb, Body and Blood b, Body and Blood c, 2Oa, 2Ob, 12Oc, 18Ob, 20Oc, 22Oa, 26Oa, 29Ob, Transfiguration

613-618 Jesus: His perfect sacrifice for us. The immense love of his Passion.

4Ac, Passion a, Passion b, Holy Thursday, Body and Blood b, 12Oc, 13Oa, 16Oc, 22Oa, 25Ob, 26Oa

624-625 Burial of Jesus and his descent into hell.

731-736 Pentecost: the Holy Spirit, God's gift.

> *3La, 6Eb, Ascension c, 7Eb, Pentecost a, Pentecost b, 17Oc*

737-741 The Holy Spirit in the Church.

> *5Eb, Pentecost b, 23Ob*

748-769 "I believe in the Catholic Church." The identity of the Church: instituted by Jesus and born of him on the cross.

> *1Aa, 3Ab, Good Friday, Easter Vigil, 4Ea, 5Eb, 6Eb, Pentecost c, 3Oc, 11Oa, 11Ob, 14Oc, 21Ob, 22Oc, 27Oa, 32Oa*

771-775 The Church: A visible reality and a hidden mystery.

> *Epiphany b, 7Eb, 5Oa, 8Ob, 9Oc, 16Ob, 21Ob, 21Oc*

781-795 The Church: The people of God and the Body of Christ with Christ as its Head.

> *Holy Thursday, 5Eb, 6Ec, Pentecost a, Pentecost c, 5Oa, 11Ob, 12Oc, 13Oa, 14Oc, 15Oc, 25Ob, 29Ob, 30Ob*

796-781 Church: Bride of Christ and Temple of Spirit.

> *7Ec, Pentecost b, Pentecost c, 8Ob, 27Oc, 28Oa, 32Oa*

811-845 The marks of the Church. The Church is one and catholic.

> *Epiphany a, 2Eb, 4Eb, Ascension a, Ascension b, 7Ec, 3Oa and, for Week of Prayer for Christian Unity, 16Ob*

823-829 The Church is holy.

> *5Lc, 7Oa, 16Oa, All Saints*

830-845 The Church is catholic. All people are called to faith in Jesus.

> *1Lb, Epiphany b, 4Eb, Ascension a, 19Oa, 20Oa, 31Ob*

846-848 "Outside the Church, there is no salvation."

> *1Lb, 4Lb, Epiphany b, 4Eb*

849-861 The Church is apostolic and missionary in its very nature.

> *Ascension a, 7Eb, Trinity b, 3Oa, 5Oc, 8Oa, 11Ob, 13Oa, 14Ob, 14Oc, 15Ob, 21Oa, 25Oc, 29Oa*

863-865 The whole Church is apostolic.

> *6Eb, 5Oc, 11Oa*

871-873 Christ's faithful: hierarchy, laity, and consecrated life.

> *4Oc, 31Oa*

874-887 Hierarchy: role of bishops in Church. The importance of the Pope and his role in the life of the Church.

> *3Oa, 3Ob, 21Oa, 27Oc, 31Oa*

888-896 Through Pope and bishops, Christ teaches, sanctifies, rules his Church.

> *3Ec, 6Ec, 7Eb, 31Oa, 30Ob*

897-913 Lay Catholics. Joy, dignity of being a Christian, and the role of the laity in the life of the Church.

> *5Ea, 4Oc, 26Oa, 30Ob*

914-919, 925-927 Religious life and the Gospel counsels. Other forms of consecrated life.

4Ob, 8Oa, 23Oc

946-953 Communion of saints: The close unity of all the faithful on earth.
2Eb, 4Eb, Pentecost c, 24Oa, All Saints

954-958 Communion of saints: Our friendship with the saints in heaven and with those in purgatory.
32Oc, All Saints

963-966 Mary: Mother of Christ, Mother of the Church.
Mother of God a, Assumption

967-970 Mary, Mother of the Church.
Mother of God c, 9Oa, Assumption

971-972 Devotion to Mary.
Immaculate Conception c

976-980 "I believe in the forgiveness of sins." The cleansing nature of baptism. The importance of the sacrament of penance.
2Ab, 2Ea, Pentecost a, 10Oa

981-983 The power of the keys. The Church's role in the forgiveness of sin.
4Lc, 24Oa

988-1004 "I believe in the resurrection of the body."
2Lc, 5La, Easter c, 2Ec, 2Ob, 6Oc, 10Oc, 14Oa, 17Oc, 18Oc, 32Oa, 32Oc, 33Ob

1005-1014, 1020 Christ's Resurrection and ours. The meaning of Christian death.
12Oa, 13Ob, 18Oa, 20Ob, 24Oa, 25Oa, 28Oc, 32Oa, 33Ob, Christ the King a, Assumption

1021, 1038-1041 Judgment: Particular and general judgments.
1Ac, 26Oc, 33Oa, Christ the King a

1023-1029 Heaven: "To live in heaven is to be with Christ."
6Oa, 32Ob, 32Oc, 33Oa, Christ the King a, All Saints

1030-1032 Purgatory.
32Oa, 32Oc

1033-1037 Hell.
12Oa, 17Oa, 21Oc, 26Ob, 33Ob, Christ the King a

1042-1050 Everlasting life: the hope of the new heaven and the new earth.
5Ec, 15Oa, 32Oa, 33Ob, Christ the King a, Christ the King b

1066-1075 Celebration of Christian faith in the liturgy.
Holy Thursday, 6Ea

1077-1109 The liturgy and the Trinity.
Holy Thursday, 1Lb, 3La, 3Lc, 2Eb, 5Eb, 6Ec, Ascension c, 7Ea, Pentecost a, Trinity a, Body and Blood b, 15Ob, 23Oa

1113-1135 Christ and the meaning of the sacraments.
3Lc, 4La, 2Ea, 5Ea, 5Eb, Ascension a, Ascension c, 7Ec, Pentecost a, Body and Blood c

1136-1144 The heavenly liturgy and the sacramental liturgy on earth.

4Ec, 5Ea, 7Ea, Body and Blood b, Body and Blood c, 11Oa, 20Ob, 22Oc, 30Ob, Assumption, All Saints

1145-1158, 1179-1186 Worship of God by his people. How the liturgy is celebrated.

Holy Family b, 3La, 5Ea, 5Ec, 3Lb, 3Oc, 9Ob, 20Ob, 23Ob

1159-1162 Holy images.

15Oc, All Saints

1163-1173 Liturgical seasons and days. The liturgical year.

Epiphany b, Easter c, 2Ea, 3Eb, 3Ec, 9Ob, All Saints

1174-1178 The Liturgy of the Hours.

20Ob

1200-1206 The rich diversity and profound unity of Catholic worship. What changes and what does not change.

Body and Blood a, 3Oc, 17Ob

1210-1212, 1229-1233 The seven sacraments of Christ and the sacraments of initiation.

Baptism of Lord b, Easter a, 13Oa

1213-1228 The sacrament of baptism. Names. Prefiguration. Christ's baptism. Baptism in the Church.

Baptism of Lord a, b, c, 1Lb, 3La, 5La, Easter Vigil, 4Ea, 4Eb, 6Eb,

Ascension b, 13Oa, 14Oc, 18Oc, 20Oc, 28Oc

1234-1252 Mystagogy of celebration of baptism. Baptism and call to faith. Baptism of adults and of children.

Easter a, 4Ea, 5Oa, 14Oc, 28Oa

1253-1274 Faith and baptism. Necessity of baptism. Graces and consequences of baptism.

2Ab, 4Lb, 5Lc, Easter Vigil, Easter b, 4Ea, 4Eb, 5Ea, 5Eb, Ascension b, Pentecost c, 2Ob, 7Ob, 18Ob

1285-1314 The sacrament of confirmation. Nature and purposes. The rites and their meaning in our lives. Who receives, and who ministers. Receiving it worthily and fruitfully.

3Ab, Baptism of Lord a, 6Ea, 6Eb, Ascension c, Pentecost a, 3Oc, 7Ob, All Saints

1322-1332 Greatness of gift of Eucharist ("the source and summit of all Christian life"). Jesus is with us most fully in the Eucharistic presence.

Holy Thursday, Easter (Emmaus Gospel), 3Ea, Christ the King a

1333-1336 Eucharist: signs of bread and wine.

Holy Thursday, 2Ob, Body and Blood a, Body and Blood c, 17Ob, 18Oa

1337-1344, 1085, 1104-1109 Jesus institutes the Eucharistic sacrifice. Makes present for us at

Christ. Sharing of all baptized in Christ's priesthood. Distinctive sharing of those who receive holy orders.

Holy Thursday, Body and Blood c, 2Ob, 30Ob

1548-1553 Christ instituted ministerial priesthood and acts in it. He calls priests to do for us good things only he can do. Priests are those who guide, teach, and sanctify in the person of Christ.

Holy Thursday, 5Oc, 30Ob

1554-1571 Bishops, priests, deacons. Orders as a gift through which Christ personally acts and teaches.

4Ob, 5Ob, Body and Blood b

1577-1580 Vocation, or call, is not a right. While only men can be called to priesthood, this is no failure to reverence the dignity of women. The importance of the gift of celibacy.

3Ob, 4Ob

1581-1589 A priest forever: sacramental character and enduring grace. The mark of Christ affects the priest as it affects all Christians in baptism and confirmation.

6Ob

1544, 1566-1569, 1587 Priesthood and the Eucharist. Christ working through his priest makes himself and his saving sacrifice present to us.

Body and Blood c, 5Ob

1601-1611 The sacrament of marriage: God the author of marriage. There is a greatness of the vocation to married life in Christ.

2Oc, 8Ob, 10Oc

1612-1617 Christ loved marriage and married people, and called them to great lives. He raised marriage to a sacrament.

Easter Vigil, 2Oc

1618-1620 Virginity for the sake of the kingdom.

3Ob, 23Oc, 32Oa

1621-1624 Liturgical celebration of marriage.

2Oc

1625-1632 Getting married must be a free act. The importance of marriage promises, and the generous love these promises commit one to. Marriage is a call to holiness.

2Oc

1633-1637 Mixed marriages. How people can and should lead holy lives in mixed marriages. How these spouses can help each other to guard faith and generous love.

17Ob

1644-1651 Unity and indissolubility of marriage. There cannot be divorce for a sacramental marriage. Annulments recognize a lack of marriage bond necessary for the sacrament. The Church must help people enter marriages validly and with hope for success.

8Ob

1652-1654 Children and marriage: how faith rightly differs from views of many in the world. Openness to children needed for a true marriage. Why contraception and sterilization are wrong.

Holy Family c

1655-1658 Family as domestic Church. The family is meant to be holy and full of faith. Responsibilities of Christian parents.

Holy Family a

1667-1676 Sacramentals. What they are and how they can help our lives. Piety at home. Popular forms of piety.

Holy Family b, Mary, Mother of God c, Ascension b, 4Ob, 10Ob

1680-1690 Christian reflection on funerals. Remembrance, prayers for those who have died, prayers for a happy death.

10Oc, 33Ob

1691-1698 What "new life" in Christ means: "Be imitators of Christ."

3Ac, 3Lc, Pentecost b, 2Ob, 7Oa, 18Ob, 18Oc, 22Oa

1699-1709 The dignity and greatness of the human person: created in the image of God.

2Ob, 15Oa, 15Oc, 25Ob

1716-1724 Walking the paths of life with Jesus. The beatitudes. Call to seek happiness in God.

4Oa, 6Oa, 6Oc, Christ the King a, All Saints

1730-1742 The real nature and grandeur of human freedom, and the false visions of freedom. "Freedom" that destroys.

1Ab, 2Ab, 5Oa, 11Oc, 13Oc, 15Oa, 22Oc

1750-1756 What makes human acts be morally good or morally bad.

8Oc

1762-1770 Our passions and feelings. Their importance and why we must "civilize" them to serve a good moral life.

13Oc

1776-1794 The understanding of consciences as the inner voice of God planted in our hearts and how we must shape our consciences rightly.

4La, 7Oc, 17Oa

1803-1811 The meaning of virtues and how the human virtues are acquired. How they serve a good and tranquil life. How grace deepens them.

3Ac, 2Lb, 14Ob, 17Oa, 27Oa

1812-1832 Faith, hope, and love: what the theological virtues are and how they transform life.

2Lb, 5Ec, 6Eb, 7Eb, Pentecost c, 4Oc, 5Oc, 7Oa, 10Oa, 11Oa, 12Oa, 15Oc, 17Oa, 19Oc, 23Oa, 27Oa, 27Oc

1846-1861 The meaning of sin. Meaning of mortal sin. Reality and tragic commonness of mortal sin.

4Aa, 1Lc, 5Lc, Passion c, 2Eb, 10Ob, 27Oa, 28Ob

1862-1869 Venial sin weakens character and creates a proclivity to more sin. Need for confession.
4La, 5Lc, 10Ob, 28Ob

1877-1899 "We must love one another." The good person as a social being and the call for solidarity and justice.
2Ac, 6Eb, 7Oc, 13Ob

1897-1904 The true meaning of authority and our duty to obedience.
29Oa

1905-1917 The common good. Concern for the life of all. Respect for the person, for social well-being and peace. Need for personal responsibility for building a good and just society.
2Ac, 14Ob

1928-1942 Authentic social justice is rooted in respect for every person. Our equality and our differences. Human solidarity.
7Oa, 15Ob, 15Oc, 23Ob, 26Oc, 33Oa, Christ the King a

1949-1964 The moral law is not mere rules or opinions, but a natural law that is planted in our hearts and revealed by a gracious God.
3Lb, 3Oc, 9Oa, 28Ob

1965-1974 The law of the Gospel is the perfection on earth of the divine law. It is the Word of Christ. Christ guides our ways through the grace of the Holy Spirit.
6Eb, 6Oa, 6Oc, 9Oa, 11Oc, 30Oa

1987-2005, 2006-2011 Grace and justification: merit.
4Lb, Good Friday, 2Ec, 4Eb, 5Eb, Pentecost c, 3Oa, 7Oa, 8Oc, 9Oa, 10Oa, 24Ob

2012-2016 Christian holiness. God calls each one of us to lead a great life, a life of great hope.
3Ab, 1Lc, 7Oa, 14Oc, 15Ob, 17Oa, 30Oc

2030-2046 The Church is our mother and teacher. Obeying her and living as she teaches is obeying Christ. Precepts of the Church.
1La, 3La, 2Eb, Ascension b, 6Oa, 9Ob, 18Ob, 22Oa, 23Oa

2050-2074 The greatness of the Ten Commandments, "the privileged expression of the natural law." The Ten Commandments flow from the two commandments of love: to love God and neighbor.
3Lb, 5Eb, 6Oa, 15Oc, 23Oa, 28Ob, 30Oa

2083 The Commandments: First, love God.
31Ob

2084-2159 The first two Commandments. Love and worship only the Lord your God and keep his name holy.
1Lc, 3Lb, 3Lc, Passion b, 4Ea, 7Ea, 6Oc, 8Oa, 9Oa, 10Oa,

2488-2499 Respecting truth in honoring secrets and in handling wisely the mass media. Addressing bias and prejudice.

13Oc, 16Ob

2500-2502 Truth, beauty, and sacred art.

20Oa

2514-2527 Ninth Commandment: Purity within the heart and thoughts. Modesty and other gracious defenses of pure love.

2Ab, 2Ac, Pentecost b, 8Oc, 11Oc, 13Oc

2534-2550 Tenth Commandment: Avoiding the avarice that a consumer society stirs up. Embracing a poverty of spirit.

7Ec, Pentecost b, 4Oa, 6Oc, 8Oa, 13Oc, 18Oc, 22Oc, 23Oc, 24Ob, 25Ob, 25Oc, 32Ob

2558-2589 The gift of prayer. Its meaning and the universal call to prayer.

Baptism of Lord b, Epiphany a, 1Lc, 2La, b, c, 3La, b, c, 4La, Easter Vigil, Trinity c, 2Ob, 9Oc, 10Oc, 14Ob, 16Oa, 16Oc, 17Oc, 18Oa, 19Ob, 19Oc, 20Oa, 20Ob, 22Oa, 24Oc, 29Oc, 30Oa, 30Oc, Christ the King c, Transfiguration

2598-2619 Christ: model of prayer and teacher of prayer.

1Ab, 1Ac, Immaculate Conception c, Mother of God c, 2La, 2Lc, 5La, Passion a, Passion c, 6Ea, b, c, Pentecost b, Trinity c, 2Oc, 6Oa, 6Ob, 9Oa, 12Oc,

13Ob, 14Oa, 14Oc, 16Oa, 17Oc, 18Oc, 20Oa, 29Ob, 30Oc, 32Oa, Assumption

2623-2643 Major kinds of prayer: Adoration. Petition. Thanksgiving. Praise. Intercession.

1Ab, 3Ac, 3Ec, Ascension b, 7Ec, Pentecost c, Trinity a, 8Oa, 15Oa, 15Oc, 16Oa, 19Oc, 20Ob, 25Oc, 26Oa, 27Oa, 28Oc, 29Oc, 30Oc, 31Oc, All Saints

2652-2691 Sources of prayer. How we learn to pray. Family as school of prayer.

4Ac, Holy Family b, 3La, 5Lc, Pentecost c, Trinity c, 8Oa, 9Ob, 10Oa, 15Oa, 16Oa, 18Oa, 28Ob, 30Ob, 33Oa, All Saints

2697-2699 Prayer: the life of the new heart.

17Oc

2700-2719 Vocal prayer: meditation and contemplation.

25Oc, 27Oa, 31Oc

2725-2751 "The battle of prayer." Why prayer is both difficult and a joy and ways to overcome these battles.

4Lc, Holy Thursday, 6Eb, 7Ea, 7Eb, 8Oa, 16Oa, 17Oc, 19Oc, 20Oc, 25Ob, 28Oa, 28Ob, 29Oc, 32Ob

2759-2854 Praying the Our Father. The Our Father as the best summary of the Gospel. The petitions.

1Ab, 1Ac, 3Ac, 4Aa, 1La, 3Lc, 4Lc, 2Ea, 5Eb, 5Ec, 7Ea, b, c, Pentecost b, Trinity a, Trinity b, Body and Blood a, Body and Blood c, 4Oa, 6Oa, 7Oa, 8Oa, 8Ob, 9Oa, 11Oa, 14Oa, 14Oc, 15Ob, 16Oa, 17Oc, 18Oa, 20Ob, 20Oc, 21Oc, 24Oa, 25Oc, 26Oa, 26Oc, 29Ob, 31Oa, 32Ob, 32Oc, 33Oa, 33Oc, Transfiguration b

Notes

Notes

Notes

Notes

Notes

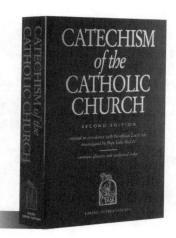

Our Sunday Visitor ...
Your Source for Discovering the Riches of the Catholic Faith

Our Sunday Visitor has an extensive line of materials for young children, teens, and adults. Our books, Bibles, pamphlets, CD-ROMs, audios, and videos are available in bookstores worldwide.

To receive a FREE full-line catalog or for more information, call **Our Sunday Visitor** at **1-800-348-2440, ext. 3**. Or write **Our Sunday Visitor** / 200 Noll Plaza / Huntington, IN 46750.

Please send me ____ A catalog
Please send me materials on:
____ Apologetics and catechetics
____ Prayer books
____ The family
____ Reference works
____ Heritage and the saints
____ The parish

Name _____
Address _____ Apt._____
City _____ State _____ Zip_____
Telephone (   ) _____
                                                                A39BBABP

Please send a friend ____ A catalog
Please send a friend materials on:
____ Apologetics and catechetics
____ Prayer books
____ The family
____ Reference works
____ Heritage and the saints
____ The parish

Name _____
Address _____ Apt._____
City _____ State _____ Zip_____
Telephone (   ) _____
                                                                A39BBABP

OurSundayVisitor

200 Noll Plaza, Huntington, IN 46750
Toll free: **1-800-348-2440**
Website: www.osv.com